Unidentified

UFO Sightings Throughout History

Julian Starling

Table of Contents

Introduction

In the 17th century in Massachusetts, the Puritan John Winthrop wrote of a strange experience a friend of his had reported to him. This friend, a man named James Everell, had been on a boat in the Muddy River when he saw a strange light that lit up the sky (Klein, 2016). More than that, he'd said that the light, when it stood still, "flamed up," but when it "ran" across the sky, it changed so that it had the appearance of a swine.

This behavior, where it ran swiftly across the sky and over a space of about two miles, continued for hours. Unbeknownst to Everell, however, he was not the only one to see this. Many other people in and around the Charlestown area saw the light do the same thing and emerged later as witnesses.

What is more, once the light had ceased its movements, Everell found himself in a strange part of the river, which would have put him against the tide. In other words, unless Everell had been rowing without conscious knowledge of doing so, he seemed to have been *moved*—although by what, he did not understand, nor could he speculate. He was, in fact, in a state of disbelief about the whole experience and hurriedly made his way home.

But what happened to Everell? Some have speculated that he had seen what is known as the *ignis fatuus*, which is a kind of pale light that emerges in swamps. It is caused by a combination of gases and decayed matter, a well-known and well-documented phenomenon.

The problem with this, of course, is that Everell, if what he reported was accurate, saw the light *in the sky*, not over the water. What about the others who claimed to have seen the same light? What about them corroborating Everell's claim that it made strange, quick movements across the sky? Surely, they had not been fooled by swamp gases—they were much too far away for that to have been the case.

But then what happened? What did they see?

Of course, we may never know the truth about what Everell saw that night. We may never know what to make of his boat's strange travel against the current or why it was that this light seemed to form itself into strange, animalistic shapes. But to modern people, it is almost impossible to read this and not have the following thought:

Is this the first American encounter with a UFO?

For some people, the idea of an early Pilgrim encountering such an object might seem unthinkable. Just the juxtaposition of primitive technology with an advanced science fiction vehicle that can traverse the stars is almost comical and surreal. After all, the current "craze" over UFOs seems to have started during the Atomic Age, when science appeared to take a quantum leap forward, and the possibility of visiting other worlds seemed like something we might actually be able to pull off.

In fact, much of the imagery around these phenomena, with their flying saucers, tripod landing gear, and aliens that emerge wearing glass domes over their heads, bring to mind movies like *Plan 9 From Outer Space* or *Mars Attacks*. They seem drawn from the well of B-movie science fiction, pulp magazines, and children's cartoons.

In other words, the idea of beings from other worlds visiting our planet seems ridiculous enough in our own time without additionally positing that early colonists in North America may have witnessed them. Every new hypothetical, it seems, brings us further into the realm of science fiction and far away from our own material, flesh and blood reality.

Except, no matter our visceral reaction to such a thing, the big question still remains: *What if it is nonetheless true?*

More so even than that: *What if these visitations have been occurring over an even longer period of time?*

What if these visitors have been appearing to us since the origin of our species?

Ridiculous? Maybe. But then again, there appear to be hints scattered throughout the historical record of strange appearances in the sky. In everything from our folklore to our religious systems and ancient literature, history is littered with references to phenomena that to us, with our contemporary eyes, appear to resemble the kind we know as a "close encounter."

Ancient and Medieval art as far back as cave paintings portray strange beings, celestial objects, and even objects that appear to be machinery. This, despite the fact that complex mechanical technology was unknown to our ancient ancestors.

Which begs the question—just where did they get the ideas for these images? Did they bubble up from the unconscious, from dreams? Or did the inspiration come in the form of a real, material encounter with something from beyond the stars?

These are the questions that used to be asked by crackpots. They were the paranoid delusions of people who were sucked down into a conspiratorial rabbit hole, only to emerge raging, frothing at the mouth, demanding to know what species of interstellar traveler was being kept in the basements at Area 51.

They could be dismissed easily, if only on the grounds that you had to be insane to think such things.

But is this the case now?

As we have advanced through the 21st century, developments in the real world have taught us that maybe we have cause to relax our skepticism. No longer, you will have noticed, are questions about alien visitors relegated to the psychotic and conspiracy-inclined. These have become topics of mainstream discussion, and for good reason.

Mounting evidence has made it look as though maybe there really have been visitors from the stars. Maybe there are things happening around us that we do not fully understand but can be explained using terms like "UFO" or "UAP." Maybe vehicles exist in this galaxy that can allow beings to traverse an unbelievable amount of space in a very short period of time.

Or maybe something else is going on entirely. Maybe something more pedestrian, more down-to-earth.

Or even something much, much stranger.

Skeptical? Well, you should be. If the UFOlogists are right, then our entire conception of our place in the universe needs to be reevaluated. The discovery, the *proof*, of alien life would indeed be the greatest discovery in the history of mankind.

These are claims that deserve to be evaluated using only the most cutting-edge tools of science. We should be able to use whatever investigative process we have available to examine these claims. Because if they can withstand scrutiny, then we know it is time to start thinking about the big philosophical questions—ones about who we are and why we are here.

Although maybe the biggest question of all has nothing to do with us and everything to do with *Them*:

Who are they? And what do they want with us?

Throughout this book, we are going to look at the UFO phenomenon from a variety of different angles. We are going to look at the experiences of people who claim to have encountered them, as well as some of the evidence cited to prove what we now know as the "ancient astronaut" theory. We will take a journey through myth and science, weaving through the tales of lights in the sky, mysterious crafts, and the quest for truth in a world brimming with the unexplained.

This is a journey with more twists and turns than you can imagine. It will take us from one end of the globe to the other as we learn just how planet-wide this phenomenon really is. We will read accounts of people from cities and farms, jungles and towns, who have seen the strange lights and gazed upon the figures that emerged from them—everyone from peasants to presidents, religious and atheists, all with something to say about what is going on in the sky.

The rocks we are about to turn over may reveal truths more horrifying than anything we could have imagined. Or they may provide us with the key to something more transcendent.

Whatever the case may be, whatever answers we uncover, things will never be the same.

Chapter 1:

Dawn of the Unexplained—Ancient Astronauts and Mythologies

In the early months of 1931, American horror writer H.P. Lovecraft produced one of the most horrifying novels in literary history: a masterpiece called *At The Mountains Of Madness*. In it, a group of explorers make a voyage to Antarctica, where they discover a long-dead city and evidence of an ancient civilization that lived there, only to vanish some millions of years ago.

Of the horrors contained in this short novel, one of the most resonant is the revelation that this ancient civilization, whose origins lay in a planet at the edge of our solar system, was not only here well before humanity existed but were themselves our creators. They made humanity, it is said, as a kind of joke before abandoning us and leaving us to our own devices.

As a young reader, this aspect of the story frightened me almost to no end. But why was this part so resonant?

In a way, the story has everything that goes into creating that palpable sense of terror that the best horror literature provides. It describes things unknown, maybe even unknowable, that occurred before recorded time. It also gives us a sense of the possibility that maybe what we understand as our history is in error—that maybe the truth of our evolution is not so much due to random chance but has been directed and guided by beings from another world.

Now, this is, of course, fiction. No interplanetary race made its home in Antarctica, so far as we know. Lovecraft's distant planet, known as Yuggoth, is a product of his own vast imagination.

And yet, in the decades since Lovecraft's time, there have been hints and whispers about the possibility that strange entities may have appeared to our distant ancestors. These hints come to us in the form of cave paintings and myths that have been recorded and preserved, which now seem to tell us of visitors from the sky.

This theory, known as the "ancient astronaut theory," is so commonly known that now it is itself a kind of folklore. It has led to reinterpretations of the Old Testament, a reexamination of the Gnostic mythologies from the 1st century, and caused us to think again about where we may have come from and to what extent we have always known the presence of creatures from beyond our planet.

But where does this idea come from? And what is the evidence for it?

Early Chronicles Of Ancient Astronauts

Other than what can be found in early 20th-century science fiction, what we know as the ancient astronaut theory really kicked off with a 1968 book called *Chariots Of The Gods?*

This book advances the thesis that aliens came to Earth long ago and influenced civilization through the introduction of technology. This means that we can break the thesis up into two parts: 1) that aliens visited the Earth in the ancient past, and 2) that they influenced the direction of history by introducing our ancestors to technology.

Starting with the first part, the writer, a man named Erik von Daniken, largely relies on reinterpretations of ancient myths, suggesting that what they describe are encounters with alien lifeforms. For example (Von Daniken, 1968):

> [T]he mythology of the Eskimos [sic] also says that the first tribes were brought to the north by "gods" with brazen wings! The oldest American Indian sagas mention a thunderbird who introduced fire and fruit to them. The Mayan legend, the Popol Vuh, tells us that the "gods" were able to recognize everything: the universe, the four cardinal points of the compass, and even the round shape of the earth.
>
> What are the Eskimos doing talking about metal birds? Why do the Indians mention a thunderbird? How are the ancestors of the Mayans supposed to have known that the earth is round? (p. 208)

First, we can poke a couple of holes in this.

The idea that ancient people did not know the Earth was round is a bizarre bit of contemporary mythology whose origin is somewhat ambiguous. However such an assumption came to be, the reality is that ancient people *did* know the Earth was round, even as far back as Ancient Greece. In fact, not only did the Greeks know the Earth was round, but they also knew approximately *how big it was.*

The Mayans were an advanced enough civilization that it is not unthinkable that they could have discerned the shape of the

Earth using methods similar, if not identical, to those of the Greeks ("looking at the horizon," for one). Surely, they did not need aliens to have told them this.

Secondly, it is hard to know how Daniken connects the idea of the thunderbird to UFOs. The thunderbird is a kind of Thor in bird form, who brings thunder and lightning using its wings for the former and its eyes for the latter. Again, how this makes Daniken think of spacecraft is beyond me unless he thinks that American Indians did not encounter birds themselves until quite recently.

Yet, there is something strangely compelling about what Daniken suggests here. Why is it that ancient religions, including Judaism and Christianity, look to the sky as the home of the gods? Why is it that the Inuit people describe their god as being made, at least partly, of metal?

Later in the same chapter, he mentions a bit of Mayan mythology regarding the return of the gods. The Mayans, it is said, calculated the moment the solar, lunar, and Venusian years would coincide, a figure which amounts to some 37k days. It was at this moment that the Mayans believed the gods would come back to Earth.

The idea that the gods are somehow connected to the planets has had more than a little resonance over the years. In our own solar system, we have named all of our own planets after the Roman pantheon, reserving the name Jupiter for the largest of these.

But believing that the passage of these planets marks when the gods will return is a stunning piece of mythology. Where did this idea come from? Even if we employ the kind of Jungian criticism that is still used in some religious circles, and we say that the Mayans resonated with it because of some unconscious association between planetary movements and the movements of the divine, we are only passing the buck here.

In other words, the source of that unconscious association is what we are looking for. Where did that story come from? And why did the Mayans believe it to be true?

As a result of the gravity of such questions and the implication that our history is not what it seems, *Chariots Of The Gods?* became an uncommon bestseller and thereby kicked off the interest in this study. But more than that, it also established the study's parameters. The search for evidence of ancient alien activity would be defined by the use and interpretation of archaeological data, as well as an examination of mythological texts, for evidence, with the assumption that these artifacts tell us of an alternative human history, one in which our trajectory was influenced by the meddling of an alien species, or perhaps several.

With these tools at their disposal, a number of researchers have exhumed and reexamined historical phenomena in light of this theory.

The results have been nothing short of astonishing.

Ancient Landing Sites, Visitors In Rock Paintings

The study of cave paintings is fascinating in itself. They seem to represent for us the first instances of consciousness truly coming alive, as our cave-dwelling ancestors sought to create representations of their thoughts and the world around them on the walls of their homes.

In the popular imagination, these paintings tend to depict animals and humans, usually as the latter hunted the former. The figures are usually simple, two-dimensional, and always shown in profile. You almost never see a cave painting of a bison looking directly at you. However, there are instances of cave paintings that seem to portray something much stranger and more haunting than these pictorial stories of men conquering nature.

A cave system in India, located 130 km outside the city of Raipur, has within it several haunting images: those of strange beings, some of them gathered together, faceless, the space behind them smudged and distorted; those of lights in the sky; and those of further beings with stout bodies, long heads, and arms that dangle well past the waist.

To look at these images is to see the uncanny. These paintings, it is said, are maybe ten thousand years old (Drolia, 2014). The locals, some of whom still worship what is in those paintings, say that their ancestors told stories of visitors from the sky who landed in round-shaped flying objects. The visitors would then take one or two of the villagers with them when they left, and those villagers would never return.

Just how old are these stories? And what *precisely* do they mean? We don't know. Again, we are faced with hints and whispers, possibilities without answer. If these stories are as old as the paintings themselves, they could be ten thousand years old. But if the stories are true, then the stories themselves should be older than the paintings still.

That would mean these people had been visited by people from the sky around the time civilization was just opening its eyes for the first time. Complex societies were in their infancy, and people were just beginning to form large cities. In other words, those stories would be *very, very old.*

Yet, given how old these stories might be, it is impossible that they did not undergo some form of alteration from their beginnings until the present. Think of how stories evolve over the famous telephone game or times when you have seen someone mythologize an event after the fact until it is barely recognizable.

It is impossible for us to keep our stories straight under any circumstances. So who knows what these ones, ones that seem to suggest alien abduction during a time when humankind was quite primitive indeed, may have looked like in their first telling?

For this reason, we may want to look to something much more concrete, something physical, that we can set our eyes on. For that, we may want to look at the Nazca lines.

Just what are the Nazca lines? Strange, geometric shapes in the desert just south of Lima. They were unknown to modern man until commercial flights soaring over them in the 1930s spotted the strange designs during their travels (History.com Editors, 2017).

What they saw was remarkable: enormous shapes etched into the ground, involving some 800+ straight lines. Some of these lines are up to 30 miles long, which is an incredible accomplishment, and they form some 300 individual designs.

The designs themselves are often simple shapes, such as squares, circles, rhombuses. But there are also wavy lines, zigzags, and arrows. The more complicated ones form various animals, which is possibly what the lines are best known for. These animals include spiders, dogs, a monkey, and a whale.

Perhaps the most interesting of all, however, is a figure known colloquially as "the Astronaut."

This figure, enormous in size, is humanoid, but in a puzzling way. He has large eyes and seems to be waving. If he is representative of a human being, it is a human being with the face of an owl. His height extends to about 40 meters.

Speculations around what this humanoid represents, of course, range in every direction one can imagine. That the figures represented in the Nazca lines tend toward the stylish, there is no doubt. The dog, for example, is a kind of exaggerated, Aztec-looking creature with embellishments around its ears and torso. The spider, while noticeably arachnid, would not be anyone's idea of a realistic portrayal of the fearsome beast.

But there is something strange about the Astronaut beyond what might be artistic embellishments or artifacts brought about by technological limitations. To the modern eye, it is impossible to look at him and not think "alien." This is what many researchers have done, of course, and speculations have run the gamut on this issue. Many to this day think that what is portrayed there is an ancient visitor from beyond whose record is kept in that gigantic and strange work of primitive art.

Making the case even stranger is that nobody has been able to figure out just why the lines were created in the first place. Here, the detail that they were first spotted by commercial airliners passing overhead is a key one. In fact, the lines themselves are *only visible from the sky*.

If they were a kind of primitive art, then the question of spectatorship becomes relevant here: Who was the intended audience for such a thing? If it was not visible to human beings during a time when nobody could see them with the naked eye, then who was supposed to see them?

The obvious answer, given what we know about primitive art, is that it had religious significance. At least one research team has speculated that the lines are related to astronomical activity, which, as we touched on briefly, had enormous religious significance for ancient people. Several more teams have rallied around the idea that the purpose of these works was to placate the gods into providing much-needed water to the region.

More recently, it has been suggested that perhaps what the lines were used for actually changed over time. Maybe at one time they were used as processional routes during religious rites, but later people adapted the lines to other, then-contemporary religious services.

The truth of the matter, however, is that we have no idea what these lines were used for. We can speculate based on what we know of other ancient religions from the South American region, but ultimately, the purpose of these drawings is elusive, possibly to such an extent that learning the truth is outright impossible.

Even spookier, perhaps, is the fact that we do not even really know *how* they were made in the first place. Sure, we know what they were made *of* because they are still standing: They were made of rocks, some from the outer regions where the Nazca tribe lived and some from further into the interior. The region being so arid is the reason why they are relatively unscathed since rain would not wear them down over time.

But how such a plan came into being is beyond the scope of our understanding. To begin with, the sheer size of these figures would make this project challenging for anyone to pull off, especially for someone with limited technology. That many of these are much more complicated than simple objects, and appear to have been the artistic renderings of the animals, for example, is what makes the task border on the impossible.

Does that mean it *is* impossible? Of course not. It is entirely conceivable that a group of people could pull off something like this, using complex planning strategies and with a religious purpose in mind.

But even still, there is a genuine mystery around how such a thing was accomplished. Coupled with the more primary mystery around their purpose and the aforementioned fact of them only being visible from the sky—it is no wonder the mind finds itself prone to speculation here.

A perceptive reader will, of course, have noticed similarities with another mysterious set of structures, which also happen to be in the desert. Like the Nazca lines, these structures have an origin, the specifics of which are unknown and surrounded by endless speculation from a variety of different camps. They come to us from a culture long buried in time and sand, even as they themselves are still standing. They are either monuments to human ingenuity or remnants of something much stranger.

We are talking, of course, about the pyramids of Giza.

The Pyramids: Keys to Life Among the Stars

The ancient Egyptian empire is one of the first civilizations in history. Although predated by Mesopotamia, it nonetheless lasted considerably longer, over a period of several millennia, and has provided Western popular culture with a far greater number of cultural references—for example, such figures as the Sphinx, mummies, and pharaohs.

Amid all of this, however—the mystery, the symbolism, the references—stand the great Pyramids of Giza.

The pyramids themselves are some 4,500 years old. For centuries, explorers and archaeologists have mapped and cataloged their interiors, particularly that of the largest one, the Great Pyramid. Perhaps because of this, they have become some of the most recognizable images in the world, somehow managing to sum up Ancient Egypt in its entirety, at least in the public consciousness.

Yet, mysteries still remain. Why were they built? *How* were they built? And do they provide further evidence that our ancient ancestors were visited and influenced by people from other worlds?

One of the more notable attempts at tackling the pyramids and their function was a 1990 book intriguingly titled *The Stargate Conspiracy*. This book begins with an explication of Egypt's mythology in the days before they became influenced by the Greek and Roman pantheons, including how the Egyptians believed that their nine gods (the Ennead) were all manifestations of a great One (Picknett and Prince, 1999). Students of Greek religion will find parallels here in how the One, which is the source of all things, emanates outward into reality—effectively, that the One becomes Many.

In any case, Picknett and Prince draw much of this from a collection of writings called the Pyramid Texts, which form the remains of ancient Egyptian funerary literature. These were the texts, in other words, that were read specifically at funerals and so incorporated much of the Egyptian religion into them. This would be analogous to how the Bible is commonly read at funerals in the West.

In fact, the Egyptian texts have much in common with the Biblical readings many of us have encountered ourselves. We might recognize the process of ascending to the presence of the godhead, for example, in addition to passages which seem to imply some version of resurrection.

However, for the writers of *The Stargate Conspiracy*, there remains a lingering question about what exactly it means to "ascend to the godhead." Do these texts, they ask, provide the key to pulling off such a feat?

What precisely would you see by the time you got there?

The book goes on to mention many of the peculiarities in the placement of the pyramids, many of which are well-known. The pyramids themselves are placed with a startling degree of astronomical accuracy, meaning they line up with stars and constellations to a degree that seems unthinkable.

Additionally, parts of the pyramid seem to indicate that the Egyptians had a much greater understanding of *pi* than may have been previously assumed. Everyone from Babylonians to early Christians had their own idea of the number behind *pi*, but the Egyptians seem to have gotten it right.

All of this, of course, is evidence for these writers that greater-than-human knowledge was at some point passed down to the Egyptians. This is something of a common theme throughout the study of ancient astronauts: namely, that the archaeological and mythological records show a level of advancement that is unlike what we expect from the historical record.

Now, regarding the supposed level of technological advancement: The explanation for why this was the case could be that ancient peoples were far more intelligent than we often give them credit for being. My own reasoning on this topic is that because of the lingering myth of progress, we assume that we are somehow far more intelligent than our ancestors were by virtue of having been born later. This is, I would argue, a false assumption.

Regarding the mythological stories, it might be that we interpret old stories in light of present-day concerns and impose an understanding on them that amounts to nothing more than a thinly stretched metaphor. For example, that we think of a "cosmic seeding" of the ingredients for life as being akin to a sexual act might be because of our tendency to think in terms of similarities and patterns, i.e., metaphors. After all, a cosmic seeding of life onto other worlds is not *literally* a sex act but is only *like* one.

But then again, the possibility that our ancestors encountered advanced technology long before they had made any of their own remains intriguing. As Picknett and Prince go on to argue, the pyramids themselves may not only provide evidence for such an encounter, but they may also present us with methods designed to put us into contact with those same space-faring people *again*.

The use of the word "stargate" in the book's title is no accident. It refers to a science fiction technology popularized by the movie *Stargate*, which was followed by a number of long-running television series, all based around the use of this device. In the most basic sense, a "stargate" is a kind of portal that can be used to travel vast distances in the time it takes to make a single step. The movie and the various shows that came after all focused on the implications of such a device and how it might be used to visit far-off worlds.

The Stargate Conspiracy posits that alien lifeforms may have used such a device. But more than that, it suggests the existence of a conspiracy in which a group of elites, at the turn of the millennium, were trying to use the device to gain access to the Ennead for their own hubristic purposes (Picknett and Prince, 1999). It is an amusing book, if only for the fact that the year 2000 has come and gone without any such thing happening.

With that in mind, it is difficult not to see the book as another in the long line of bizarre predictions from within the New Age movement about when and how the world is going to end. One thinks here of the supposed Mayan calendar end-times prophecy, which has also come and gone without any change—whether that be in consciousness, the coming of Planet X, or any other apocalyptic scenario.

Nonetheless, books like *The Stargate Conspiracy* do contain within them the seeds of how the ancient astronaut theory views the pyramids of Giza. It suggests that they contain hints of ancient contact with an unbelievably advanced civilization, which may or may not provide us with a kind of roadmap for how to make contact with these beings again.

Furthermore, the Egyptian myths, like the myths of other ancient peoples, are reinterpreted as stories of alien contact. With this in mind, if accurate, our mythological narratives are not only true in a much more concrete sense than we might commonly believe but depict for us an alternate history from the one we are taught is true.

In Summary

As we have discussed, the ancient aliens phenomenon has been discussed extensively in recent years. While it originally began as the speculation of science fiction writers like H.P. Lovecraft, it has since gone on to inspire legions of amateur archaeologists and religionists to explore existing data with the following question in mind: Is there evidence in the physical sciences, as well as in the myths of ancient peoples, that describes to us encounters with beings from other worlds?

As we can see, the answer to that is not so straightforward. But as we will soon see, it is not only the early myths of our long-ago ancestors that can be examined in light of the UFO phenomenon.

In fact, the stories of angels and demons of the next age can be subjected to the same treatment. The results of that project just might make you rethink all you know about the Middle Ages.

Chapter 2:

Roaming Skies—Medieval and Renaissance Sightings

The Middle Ages was the time of Christianity's apex in Europe. After the fall of Western Rome in the 400s, Christianity took the reins of civilization and attempted to build it back to its former glory. That it was not without its downsides is common knowledge at this point. Certainly, there is a legacy of dogmatism, paranoia, and brutality that has few rivals in the annals of history. Nonetheless, Christianity provided a common thread in terms of ethics, metaphysics, and the like, along with its institutional hierarchies, starting with lay people and working up through the ranks: priest, bishop, cardinal, and on. This hierarchy still exists in the Catholic system and in a slightly reduced aspect in the Orthodox faith.

But as Christianity flourished, so did its common mythological touchstones. The Bible, of course, is the Holy Book of the faith, with its Old and New Testaments, and so the stories of Adam and Eve, Elijah, and the Gospels were all common knowledge, at least among the literate and educated.

Beyond those better-known stories, however, came stories of other creatures that were said to wander the Earth. The Bible of course makes references to angels and demons, as well as the idea of possession by demons. These became common folk beliefs in the Middle Ages, and still persist to varying degrees into the present.

In the spirit of reevaluating the myths of the ancients, we might ask ourselves what results such a reevaluation of the stories of angels and demons might yield for us. Are these stories describing encounters with beings from the stars filtered through the common folk myths of the Medieval people? Are there similarities between alleged supernatural encounters and the modern conception of abduction by aliens? And what can the idea of demonic possession tell us about the nature of the beings who might inhabit the far regions of our galaxy?

Aliens and the Bible

It is important to start with this subject, that of aliens in the Bible, for a variety of reasons. To begin with, the Bible's influence on the Middle Ages was so pervasive that no account of that period of history can be written without taking that influence into account. It was, for all intents and purposes, *the* reference for all of that period's written works.

However, for our purposes, the most important thing to consider about that collection of books is that it can be interpreted as presenting evidence for alien visitations. This will require us to jump around in time a bit, but if we can establish that the Bible is amenable to this interpretation, then when we go through some Medieval writings, legends, and so forth, we should find new dimensions to those works than we would have otherwise.

With that in mind: Many interesting and eccentric books have been written on this topic, so it is not exactly obvious which one we should start with. Given that this is also something of a fringe subject, it is a challenge to determine which of these books is more "credible" than the other.

That issue of credibility, however, is what led me to pursue a book called *The Bible And Flying Saucers*. To begin with, it is the source of some of the most revisionist claims about the Biblical stories, to such an extent that it sees a significant number of them as being about the influence of alien life on our species. Since it takes this extreme view, it is illustrative of the interpretive possibilities contained within the Bible, and so lays the groundwork for further interpretation.

More than that, the book was written by a man named Barry Downing, who is himself a Presbyterian minister and has been featured a number of times on the History Channel show *Ancient Aliens*. So, while his claims might lean toward the outlandish, he is nonetheless educated on the Bible and could be considered a credible source on its interpretation, so far as that goes.

Regarding his interpretations in themselves, he makes some genuinely idiosyncratic suggestions on how to read the Bible. For example, he refers to the book of Exodus, in which Moses and the Israelites are visited by the Lord, who comes down from a cloud. This same figure then follows—or, rather, *leads*—the Jewish refugees through the desert after their escape from Egypt. This, he says, is clear evidence that the Israelites were "led by a UFO" (Downing, 1973).

It is, however, his readings of the New Testament which are perhaps the most radical. Regarding the life of Jesus of Nazareth, Downing is keen to regard him as a kind of "undercover agent" sent by the people from another world (Downing, 1973). He even muses at one point at the strangeness of this decision on the part of the extraterrestrials—after all, "angels" (read: "aliens") are, in the New Testament, said to be powerful to a rather astonishing extent. That they chose to send this undercover agent must, he writes, have come from a desire to undermine our trust in worldly governments.

The ascension of Christ too seems to provide further evidence of his alien origin. In the Gospel of John, it is said that strange beings were seen around the empty tomb, commonly understood to have been angels. When Christ is finally taken into heaven, after the Resurrection, he is said to have been taken up by a bright cloud.

For Downing, this is clear evidence that Jesus was, in fact, carried off into space by a UFO. Not just any UFO, but the same UFO that led Moses and the Israelites through the desert, took Elijah into the heavens, and descended like a "dove" after Jesus' baptism by John.

Paul's conversion is also connected to the UFO phenomenon. As Downing states, such an event could only be compared to a hypothetical in which Adolf Hitler defected to the Allies during WWII—such was the horror of Paul's persecution of early Christians. His conversion story involves encountering Jesus on the road to Damascus, whereupon Jesus asks Paul why he (Paul) is persecuting him (Jesus). This leads to Paul's change of character, after which he becomes the church's first theologian and perhaps its greatest apostle.

Downing's take on this will not be surprising. He says that the same vehicle which brought Jesus into the heavens came down once again, to place Jesus before Paul. Because of this intervention, Christianity gains an adherent that allows it to spread to a much larger audience than it would have had Paul (then known as Saul) continued his hunt for believers in Christ.

In other words, Downing's idea is that the whole tradition of Judaism through to Christianity has its origins in alien visitations. Not only that, but the spread of Christianity at the end of the Roman Empire and especially through the Middle Ages means that humanity has shared with its brethren a message given to them by an alien being. The religion with more adherents than any other in the history of the world is an alien religion involving the worship of an extraterrestrial.

All of this shows, I think, that the Christian Bible is amenable to the same kind of reinterpretation as the ancient myths we discussed in the previous chapter. But just how far can we extend this? Can the experiences of Medieval people—experiences they interpreted through the lens of Christianity—be understood instead as encounters with UFOs?

Lights in the Sky

The experience of seeing strange lights in the sky was much more common in the Middle Ages than one might at first think. One book, titled *Wonders In The Sky* by Jacques Vallee and Chris Aubeck, details an unbelievable number of them throughout all of history. However, there is an enormous section of Medieval sightings in that book, which follow a similar, even *identical,* pattern to the stories we hear today.

For example, Saint Benedict of Nursia claims to have risen one morning to say his matins while it was still dark. As he did, he saw a light so bright that it was greater than the light of day and banished the darkness of the early morning (Vallee and Aubeck, 2010).

Once he adjusted his eyes to the brightness, he saw that within the light was the soul of a bishop named Germanus, who was being carried by angels up to the heavens. Interestingly, Benedict had not yet heard of Germanus' death, but this fact was confirmed upon inquiry.

Another interesting encounter is contained within the *Annals of Ireland.* As Vallee and Aubeck note, it is an illustrative story from that period in that several accounts, along with this one, relate the experience of seeing "shields" in the sky (Vallee and Aubeck, 2010). In this particular account, three of these shields are described as undulating around the sky, almost as waves or as if "warring" with one another. They are also understood as having something to do with the Ascension of the Lord, which is a fascinating bit of interpretation, coming from the year 698, quite some time before Downing made a similar connection.

About fifty years later, in 749, another report from Ireland states that a ship was seen in the sky (Vallee and Aubeck, 2010). But what separates this one from the others is that not only was the ship itself seen, but allegedly, so was the *crew*.

There are no more details on what precisely was meant by this. There are no descriptions of what the crew looked like nor what kind of ship was seen. Nonetheless, the account states that beings of some type were seen piloting a ship that was in the air.

Then, in 776, after a series of failures, Charlemagne made an attempt at storming the castle at Sybrug, Germany (Vallee and Aubeck, 2010). As his army ran in the direction of the castle, however, two *shields* appeared over the fortress as if in its defense. The appearance of these objects was enough to horrify Charlemagne's army into fleeing, which led to their impalement upon the lances of their own men.

This is an extraordinary account for a variety of reasons. First, that these shield-like objects intervened successfully in a war makes this a different sort of encounter than the more passive ones we have discussed thus far. In the others, the objects are seen almost, it seems, by happenstance: Someone is going about their business, only to have their attention directed upwards by the strange movements of these lights overhead. The Syburg incident, however, is one in which they appear with what appears to be a purpose in mind, or, at least, that their appearance has an effect on a particular outcome.

The other, of course, is that the soldiers themselves interpreted this event and the subsequent impalements as signs of divine retribution (Vallee and Aubeck, 2010). Here, again, is the idea that this phenomenon has a connection to the mythological and metaphysical claims of Christianity—in this case, that God has intervened in the affairs of men to punish them for their transgressions in war.

The book *Wonders In The Sky* goes on to detail many more stories of this type over the entire Medieval period. In nearly every one of them, someone, usually a religious, military, or political figure, sees something bright in the sky that makes strange movements, or has the appearance of a shield. Always, the witness describes it in Christian terminology, but in particular the object is most often described as being an "angel."

But what precisely did Medieval people mean by terms like "angel" or "demon?" Just how closely do these concepts resemble our own beliefs around aliens and, especially, the phenomenon of abduction?

St Thomas and the Angelic Order

The great philosopher of the Catholic Church, St Thomas Aquinas, is a towering figure in Western history. His contributions to metaphysics, ethics, theology, and natural law are perhaps unparalleled in their scope and the depth of their insight. His magnum opus, an enormous work titled *Summa Theologicae*, covers virtually every aspect of Medieval thought, from questions about the existence of God all the way to questions about what it means to legislate, what a person is, how to read the Bible, and countless others.

But it is his writings on angels and demons that are of particular interest to us. Alas, Thomas' own writings on the subject take up many pages, and a proper explication of his beliefs might take up many books of their own. So we will have to examine them briefly, but especially in how he understands the relationship between angel or demonic beings and man.

Regarding what precisely angels and demons *are*, Thomas says that they are "intellectual creatures," meaning they are pure intellect, i.e., not made of matter (Magee, 2020). This was something of a debate in Thomas' time, as some of his colleagues believed in what was called "universal hylomorphism," which is to say that some things were made of matter, but angels were made of "spiritual matter." Thomas thought this was a confused term, as "spiritual," by definition, means "not material."

Contrary to how these beings are conceived in storytelling, St Thomas, and by extension, Catholic philosophy after him, believed that they were not material beings and so could be comprehended by the senses. Therefore, any depiction of them as malformed, monstrous creatures, often as combinations of mismatched beings such as flies and frogs, is an artistic rendering of something that cannot be put into images.

But while this in itself excludes the possibility that aliens might be some type of angelic beings since aliens, by definition, would be made of matter, it is in how Thomas understood angels to affect people that we run into some interesting points of contact.

The shortest version of his thoughts on the subject runs something like this: A human being has his own free will, such that he makes choices for himself (Aquinas, 2020). These choices, however, are influenced by various things, such as what he called "the passions," which are your emotions. In other words, a person who experiences anger can be moved to make a choice out of anger. This does not mean that anger made the choice for him but that he allowed his anger to persuade him of something and then acted upon it.

Angels, he says, can "rouse" the passions. This means they can cause you to experience feelings of anger, love, jealousy, whatever, and having done so can cause you to make decisions based on that emotion's influence.

What is most interesting, however, is that Thomas says an angel can cause what we would term a "hallucination." They can influence our minds such that we see something that is not there and then make a free decision based on whatever we are hallucinating. In this way, we can be influenced by spiritual beings who deceive our senses.

How this relates to the Medieval conception of miracles is interesting also. For Thomas, a miracle was not something like a break in the laws of nature. It was, rather, one of two things: Either it was something we did not have an explanation for (but something for which an explanation was possible), or it was something that caused us to experience astonishment. Notice that at no point does he suggest that miracles are things that cannot make sense—they are, rather, something beyond our then-current ability to understand.

For a Medieval person, then, an experience that roused astonishment due to its apparent (but not really) break with the natural order, which caused a person to see things that were not there and to feel emotions that seemed foreign to them, was a sign of angelic or demonic influence.

This, of course, applies to something like "seeing a pair of shields descend from the sky." How such a thing could be possible was not something a Medieval person could answer—frankly, if that were literally true, there is not a soul in the history of the planet who would have an answer ready for such a thing. For all intents and purposes, it appears miraculous or else is the product of something toying with one's senses. What else could do that except for an angel or a demon?

With that in mind, it is time to look at a possible comparison. For this, we are going to bring another book into the conversation. This is one titled *Abductions—Human Encounters With Aliens*, by a man named John E. Mack, M.D. This is a book-long study of the abduction phenomenon by a psychiatrist, in which he examines and reports on the alleged experiences of abductees.

For our purposes, the information we need from it has to do with what exactly people claim to go through when they have this experience. In other words, what does an abduction feel like? What kind of effect do alleged alien beings seem to have on the people that are abducted? And what is the connection with St Thomas?

The first thing to make mention of here is that there are a number of recurring patterns that Mack has identified, with regards to the experience itself. The whole list is much too long for a summary here, but there are quite a few elements that stand out for the purposes of this discussion.

For example, he says that many people, as the abduction sequence begins, feel strongly that there is an otherworldly "presence" nearby (Mack, 1999, p. 14). They tend to feel that their bodies are vibrating right around the time they see a bright light. At some point, they see up close what they interpret to be a UFO, which they are taken inside of. The beings that they find inside the craft are either benevolent or malevolent, although often, beings that appear benevolent, especially in childhood, reveal themselves later to be quite evil.

After returning from the alleged abduction, the abductees sometimes have bruises or markings on them and react with anxiety to stimuli that would not have given them that feeling before. For example, someone might all of a sudden develop a feeling of fear around the sound of a blender, which appears to have come from nowhere.

But there is another element, or rather a series of elements, that are perhaps most interesting here. Many abductees claim that the alien beings provide them with information or inculcate changes in the abductee's consciousness. This is done through telepathy, such that the alien can make someone experience an emotion quite deeply, simply through psychic abilities.

Furthermore, the aliens often explain to the abductees that they need to return with a message or at least are given information about the alleged fate of mankind. For example, they might be told that nuclear warfare will wipe us all out, that we need to end climate change, or that some technology we have developed will lead to our ruin in some way. To do this, the aliens show the abductee images of nuclear holocaust, for example, as a kind of warning of what may lay ahead.

Now, as Mack states, the purpose of such a revelation might have two purposes. In the first, it might be the case that alien beings are indeed looking out for our best interests and giving us information that would help us in the long run.

But the second—and Mack says this is an opinion he has encountered before—it might be that the aliens are trying to actively deceive us. Given that their warnings tend to be about advanced technology, it might be that they are encouraging a kind of deceleration of human civilization in order to make us more vulnerable.

For myself, as a reader, there was one sentence in particular that stood out, and it was this: "They [the researchers into abduction experiences] argue further that if the aliens were truly concerned with our well-being, they would manifest themselves more forthrightly and intervene directly in our affairs in order to make things better" (Mack, 1999, p. 25).

The notion that aliens—beings that are much further advanced than we are and who come from the stars—would, if they were truly benevolent, *intervene on our behalf* to save us from destruction is perhaps the greatest indication of religious overtones in UFO research. Furthermore, the idea that malevolent aliens would deceive us in order to make us vulnerable appears to take the common conceptions of angels and demons and give them gray alien masks.

But of course, that is not the only possibility. In fact, it might be that the influence runs the other way. As we have seen, St Thomas, *the* great philosopher of the Middle Ages, understood angels and demons to be creatures who could arouse in us certain passions in order to influence our will. In many of the experiences we have talked about so far, Medievals reported seeing strange lights in the sky, which Mack says are absolutely associated with abductions. It certainly seems as though beings who concerned themselves with worldly affairs and attempted to influence us with regard to warfare and violence appeared to Charlemagne's army in Germany.

In essence, connections between the two are not as flimsy as they might at first appear.

A Space Battle Over Renaissance Germany

The final element to discuss here is that of a fascinating woodcut from the year 1561.

This woodcut first became known to the public through Carl Jung's work *Flying Saucers: A Modern Myth of Things Seen In The Sky* (Colavito, 2012). In it, we see bizarre objects in the skies, which appear to be in motion. At the bottom, townspeople look upon the scene, and the size of buildings provide scale for the celestial objects—basically, they show that the things in the sky are enormous.

On the one hand, it has been suggested that this is an artistic representation of a "sundog," which is when sunlight hits atmospheric ice and is refracted out into the sky. On the other, sundogs tend to be, yes, bright lights in the sky, but not geometric shapes like the ones in the woodcut.

Might these just be artistic representations of a particularly bright sundog? Certainly. On the other hand, it has been suggested amongst various UFO research groups—and other, even more maligned groups, if you can imagine such a thing—that what is depicted is an actual UFO battle taking place over Renaissance Germany.

That this theory has not gained credence outside of publications like *The Weekly World News* (which is itself a parody of tabloid journalism, famous for its long-running updates on a character named Bat Boy) makes the possibility that a UFO battle took place at that time perhaps slightly less likely. However, the woodcut itself does remain a strange bit of history, perhaps drawing our attention to the likelihood that visitations from alien races took place not just during the ancient period and our own but all throughout our species' time on this Earth.

Instances of UFOs appearing in art from that period—and into the Renaissance—are far more common than one might at first think. For example, Masolino da Panicale's painting *The Miracle Of The Snow* (c. 1428–32) shows an incident from Catholic legend regarding the founding of the Roman Basilica Santa Maria Maggiore (Artnet News, 2023). As the legend states, the basilica's site was chosen by Mary, who caused snow to fall on it—an admittedly rare occurrence in sunny Rome.

However, in depicting this, Panicale's painting shows something quite curious to modern eyes. In it, the Pope and several Roman figures stand at the site of what would become the Basilica, but overhead, Jesus and Mary appear in what is perhaps supposed to be a large cloud grouping, but to us now appears to be a fleet of UFOs. The clouds themselves are gray and shaped in the way that a classic UFO is often depicted, slightly flat near the edges and round.

Another curious one is Jacques Legrand's Livre des Bonnes Meurs (c. 1430), an illuminated manuscript meant to teach people good manners. One image shows people gathered around Fortuna and her wheel—a common enough image in Western history. Overhead, however, is a gold sphere floating in the sky. The finer details of this sphere make it appear to be mechanical, which is interesting enough on its own. But even if we consider this an interpretive imposition, what is the sphere meant to depict? Where do glowing spheres of that type feature in Medieval legend or folklore? Is it perhaps meant to echo Ezekiel's visions?

But the most famous of all of these paintings is undoubtedly Domenico Ghirlandaio's *Madonna with Saint Giovannino* (c. 15th century). This is the painting in which the Madonna is seen praying over the infants Jesus and Saint John. But a strange detail in the background has led to the painting being referred to as the "Madonna dell'UFO."

Over Mary's left shoulder, hovering in the blue sky, is a blob; at least, this is maybe the most uncontroversial word for what the artist chose to decorate the sky with. It is greenish colored, it floats in the sky amongst the clouds, and there is absolutely nothing, no reference within the painting, to indicate just what this is supposed to represent.

Yet, the artist chose to incorporate that image into the piece. So why did he do this? Why did he choose to have a floating, spherical object float in the sky at the time of Jesus' birth?

In Summary

The Middle Ages was home to a wide variety of myths, folklore, and beliefs regarding strange and often spiritual beings who could visit us, create changes in our perceptions, and influence us to do their bidding. In the ancient period, these powers were proscribed to gods and goddesses, but in the Medieval period, this was said to be the province of angels and demons. Other creatures from folklore—fairies and so forth—were also implicated but were not discussed here.

If, in the previous age, it was possible that people misinterpreted the acts of technologically advanced beings to be those of gods, then the possibility surely must extend to the age after the fall of Rome. Given the similarities between abduction experiences and encounters with angels, could it not be that they are one and the same?

There were more things we could have gotten into had we had the time. Various paintings beyond our famous woodcut seem to show levels of technology unknown to the people of that time.

But given all this, can we not imagine that perhaps our Medieval ancestors were themselves visited by things they did not understand? Is it not possible that they, too, saw things in the sky from other worlds? Certainly, that is how they described their experiences, but they used the language of their own time.

Are we not doing the same thing? Are we not describing these things as aliens or vehicles—words drawn from the sciences, the dominant way of assessing the world in our own time? How will people in our future describe their own encounters?

Before we get there, we need to make a few pit stops. The first of those is to the Victorian Age.

Chapter 3:

Phantom Airships of the 19th Century—A Premonition of Flight

The late Victorian Age was a time of rapid change. In England, the terror of Jack the Ripper brought tabloid journalism into its modern form and gave us the first case of what we now call the "serial killer." Industrialization was near its peak, and scientific innovation, mixed with a Romantic interest in the occult—particularly seances—spurred the imaginations of a great many denizens of that era.

In fiction, two writers—one English and one French—all but invented the genre we now call "science fiction," with their stories of Martian invasions, trips to the moon and around the world, and genetic modification. The works of H.G. Wells and Jules Verne can be said, in many ways, to represent the forward-thinking nature of people at the time, a people fascinated by the possibilities of science.

Their dreams have become our reality in many ways, but it is crucial to note that the idea of flying around the world in 80 days was considered somewhat outlandish at the time of *Around The World In Eighty Days*' publication (after all, what sense is there in writing a novel about a feat that can be easily accomplished?). That novel predates the Wright brothers' first flight by several decades but roughly coincides with the time when Zeppelins were first conceived of.

All this to say that while the Victorians imagined fictional worlds in which flying could be accomplished by a single passenger, this was not yet a commonplace reality by the time of the late 19th century.

So, how was it that so many Americans and British claimed to have seen "airships" flying across their skies beginning in November 1897?

Because that is what happened: A large number of people saw what were declared "airships" passing through the skies, shining searchlights down on the world below. It was seen not just by cranks but by reputable people. While it was seen one day over Sacramento, it was seen the next night in San Francisco. That would be an enormous distance to cover at that speed with the technology available.

But then it was seen in the Midwest. Then it was seen in England.

Then, just as quickly as it began, it ended.

To date, several explanations have been offered for how such a thing came to be—although few doubt that such a thing *did*, in fact, happen. The lack of a solid answer on the subject only makes the mystery more compelling, but the details of what happened alone are quite terrifying in themselves.

Still, what was it that these people saw? How could such a thing happen?

What does it say about our reality?

The Events

Sacramento in 1897 was a town of roughly thirty thousand or so residents (Danelek, 2009, chapter 1). The evening of November 17 was a gloomy one. As is typical of central California in the late autumn, there were low clouds and a few squalls along with a terrible chill in the air. Beyond this, however, the day had been relatively uneventful.

Much to everyone's surprise, then, an event of terrible significance did, in fact, occur. Somewhere around eight o'clock, an object came over the eastern horizon, flying high. It traveled slowly toward the west and shone a light that resembled a kind of searchlight. Eyewitnesses who first saw the thing come over the horizon said that the light appeared to be on the bottom of a dark mass. This mass was later described as "cigar-shaped."

From there, however, accounts of the thing's appearance vary. Some witnesses said it had enormous propellers. One said it had huge paddles all along each side of it. Still another said that he saw the craft being operated by human occupants, who kept the craft in the air by pedaling furiously on bicycle pedals.

But while certain descriptions clearly border on the outlandish, all who saw it agreed on the existence of that bright light on its bottom. There were indeed dozens who saw it that night, especially as it passed over the capitol building. There, it was even seen by an assistant to the Secretary of State of California.

Then, half an hour after its appearance, the ship—or whatever it was—disappeared into the gloomy sky. Just as it had come in, it went away.

But what was it? And where did it come from?

Immediately, the newspapers jumped on the story. They made it the front page and ran stories for several days of speculation on the strange event. The two biggest papers in the state, *The*

Sacramento Bee and *The San Francisco Caller* published numerous accounts by alleged witnesses describing the storied events.

As one can imagine, this led to a flood of "witnesses," many of whom came forward with stories that simply could not be true. (The one about the craft being pedaled as if a giant bicycle, for example.) Perhaps because of this, the public was keen to dismiss the whole episode as being caused by "tom foolery"—or, in modern terms, "getting absolutely hammered."

The story, however, refused to die. Not only did the papers continuously push the issue to the front page, but people would not stop talking about it. It really was "the talk of the town."

Then the unthinkable happened—the ship appeared *again.* Only this time, it appeared to considerably more witnesses and in more than one city.

It appeared in both of those cities *on the same night.*

The date of the second appearance was five days later, on November 22nd. This was a Sunday, which meant more people were out and about, which meant more possible witnesses. According to records at the time, the weather was much the same as it had been five days previous: gloomy, overcast, and cold.

It was during the evening that the ship appeared again. This time, the deputy sheriff and the district attorney were counted among the witnesses. All of these townspeople watched the craft for nearly half an hour as it floated noiselessly across the sky with its mysterious searchlight.

Then, only a few hours later, it appeared again—except this time in San Francisco.

It did appear there. Not only were there hundreds of witnesses, but among those was the city's mayor. It was even alleged that the searchlight frightened a group of seals enough to cause them to leap into the Bay. This would mean the ship traveled a distance of about 80 miles in a single night—a considerable distance by any measure but seemingly impossible to pull off given the technology of the time.

From there, the story became a sensation. It appeared in newspapers all over the Pacific, drawing all manner of speculation from the people who lived nearby. Interestingly, this speculation was not centered around whether or not the craft was a threat, which would certainly be the expected response. Instead, everyone wanted to know what is perhaps a much more frightening question: *Who was piloting the thing?*

As one can imagine, all manner of people came forward with answers. There were people who claimed they knew of mysterious and reclusive billionaire inventors who had put together such a machine, funded using their own money and resources. One man, a lawyer named William Henry Hart, claimed that there were in fact two airships, which would soon be used to bomb Havana. (Cuba was, at the time, the subject of a territorial dispute between the Americans and the Spanish.)

Despite this, nobody was able to point conclusively to anyone who had piloted, built, or funded the creation of this ship. Speculation went on in the press for a month or so before interest waned and the stories disappeared.

But just as it disappeared, the ship began to appear again. This time, it was over Nebraska, then again over Iowa. From there, it was spotted all over the Midwest and into Texas. Newspapers all over that part of the country reported sightings from all manner of people and featured all manner of descriptions of the craft itself.

Of course, the "cigar-shaped" descriptor came up a number of times. Still others said the ship had wings and feathers. The more fantastical stories were from people who claimed to have met the pilots of the craft, who were described as human (or human enough to pass for one of us), and who were quite willing to discuss the ins and outs of the ship. Some too claimed that they were given tours of the vessel.

Eventually, the ship made it to Illinois, where it was spotted over Chicago. One man said he'd taken a photograph of it, although the photograph was never showcased to the public. From there, the craft continued into Michigan, where it appeared over Kalamazoo.

There was a lot of buzz about where the ship was ultimately headed. Could it be New York? Philadelphia? And what would its final destination reveal about the nature of the craft's journey? Or would the crew reveal themselves at that point, in a dramatic fashion, and announce to the world what it was they had done?

Alas, such a "go out with a bang" ending never came to be. Some local papers in New York State reported the ship over Yonkers, but that story never made the front page of any of the biggest American papers. Instead, the ship did not surface again, and the papers merely let the story die.

But what *did* happen? Was anything ever revealed about whether there was such a craft? Given enough hindsight, what can we say conclusively about what had happened in the American skies near the turn of the previous century?

The Answers

Unfortunately, whatever answers we might hope for may never be answered. Nothing was proven then, and all we have now are old newspaper reports and scattered other documents saying that a remarkable thing appeared to happen before the likely thousands of witnesses across the continental United States. But of those reports, little can be made.

Why is this? Partly, it has to do with what was once called "yellow journalism," meaning sensationalized, often untrue "news" stories that rely less on reporting the facts to an interested public and more on selling newspapers. These practices were commonplace at the end of the 19th century, which leaves the facticity of the reports on the airship in doubt (Danelek, 2009).

In essence, this theory suggests that the airship and everything else about it was nothing more than a newspaper hoax. In fact, the newspapers may have "poisoned the well," so to speak, by relaying information about what the ship was supposed to look like, thereby encouraging eyewitnesses to interpret, say, the shining light of Venus as a cigar-shaped, flying piece of technology equipped with a working searchlight.

However, this explanation is unsatisfying. As Danelek points out, "yellow journalism" has a particular set of goals it tries to achieve, which would make a hoax about an airship something of a novelty (2009). Consider, for example, the newspaper mogul William Randolph Hurst, the father of yellow journalism himself. He used his news empire to inflame patriotic support—essentially, to engineer public opinion—against the Spanish to justify going to war with them. To do this, he exaggerated reports about Spanish atrocities taking place in Cuba, effectively making war unavoidable.

Notice, however, that Hurst was trying to steer public opinion toward a certain belief (the Spanish are evil) in order to obtain a goal (war with the Spanish). What precisely would the goal have been with regard to the airship? There was no political motivation, certainly. So, what were the papers trying to accomplish?

The charge can be levied against them that they were merely trying to sell papers, effectively operating as a tabloid. There is some evidence that the papers were "giving the people what they want" since they stopped printing stories about it after public interest waned. Some of the stories can be dismissed with greater aplomb than others—for example, the same airship was allegedly seen in both Texas and the Dakotas on the same night.

The sheer number of newspapers who printed the story should make us pause as well. The idea that they could have all been working on the same hoax at the same time, without any of that information leaking, strains credulity. It is a fact that has hampered conspiracy theories since time immemorial, namely that people like to blab—especially if it helps them get ahead. Selling secrets to a rival newspaper in exchange for the editor-in-chief job is certainly a way to do that.

But mostly, a newspaper relies on its reputation in order to make money. Not even a sensationalized headline can get someone to buy a paper that is known for printing utter nonsense—unless they, the consumer, are more or less in on the joke. (This might apply to the *National Enquirer*.) Major newspapers especially have a lot to lose if they are seen as disreputable. So, while journalists at the time may have engaged in what we now call "yellow journalism," they still had to inform the public to a degree that kept their reputation intact. Going along with a nationwide hoax in order to sell papers would stop them from reaching that goal.

But if a nationwide newspaper hoax can plausibly be ruled out, what are we to make of the possibility that these events involved visitors from space?

The Alien Hypothesis

First, the evidence against: Very little about these craft suggests that they are related in any way to what we know of as UFOs. That they tended to be slow should cause us to raise some eyebrows, as UFOs, at least those we are accustomed to hearing about today, are generally thought of as fast-moving. While some UFOs are described as "cigar-shaped," very few of them are said to have searchlights on the bottom.

Furthermore, it is hard to imagine how these slow-moving ships could have traversed the galaxy in order to wind up here. The nearest star to us, Alpha Centauri, is still extraordinarily far away, such that a slow-moving craft would take several lifetimes to cross that distance. If these airships were capable of moving any faster, nobody saw them do such a thing. In other words, there is no evidence of them being capable of fast travel, and so we cannot assume that they would be.

Yet, if they are not UFOs, what else could they possibly be? Do we rule this possibility out simply because the objects in question do not conform to our expectations of what a UFO should be?

In fact, we might use this case to test some of our assumptions about the UFO phenomenon. One of the questions we might ask ourselves is why we assume these objects have traveled across vast, interstellar distances. Could they not, at least some of them, come from Earth, even if the pilots themselves are not?

There is one more wrinkle here that we need to examine before we move on. A newspaper out of Aurora, Texas, reported that one of these airships—if indeed there were more than one, which is not impossible—crashed into a windmill and burned (Danelek, 2009). The reporter on the scene said that the pilot of this craft had been badly burned, but there was enough left for him to make a chilling observation.

According to the reporter, there was enough left of the pilot's remains to determine that its origin was not from this world.

That is not all. The reporter states that the craft itself seemed to bear markings that reminded him of hieroglyphs. He said, too, that the craft was made of a mysterious metal that nobody in town could identify. Finally, he assured his readers that he would give the poor fellow a proper Christian burial.

If that sounds implausible, it will not help the man's case that he also supposedly took the remains to an astronomer friend of his, who proclaimed that this being was clearly from Mars. At the time, it was not common knowledge that Mars is a barren wasteland, so the idea that aliens might live on our neighboring planet was not so far-fetched. (Consider *The War Of The Worlds*.)

However, sometime in 1973, a group of researchers from MUFON (Mutual UFO Network) heard about the crash and did some digging. In particular, they wondered about the reporter burying the airship pilot. Did he actually do this? Or was this just part of the yarn he spun?

If he did—was the grave still there?

What they found was more than a little interesting: In the Aurora cemetery, there existed a grave with a curious marking over it. It had no name and no date—but it was marked with a rock, which had an image chiseled into it.

An image that appeared to be of an airship.

The researchers at MUFON petitioned the local government to allow them to excavate this grave, perhaps accurately assuming that if there really was an alien being buried there, that it would be the most significant find in human history. However, the local government denied the request, not wanting a UFO research group digging all through their cemetery looking for aliens.

Despite this, the cemetery was flooded with UFO enthusiasts for some time, all wanting to see the grave which housed an alien being. Although eventually the enthusiasm fizzled out, one more strange thing was to take place.

At some point, the grave marker went missing. Whether from vandals or someone else, nobody knows. It could have been that someone wanted a souvenir. Or it could have been that someone was trying to get rid of an identifying mark to keep people from snooping around.

Whatever the reason, they did not get rid of whatever was under that dirt. To this day, that grave sits there, unmarked in the Aurora cemetery.

You can visit it any time you like.

The Aftermath

As quickly as the airships arrived, they disappeared. Like a figment of the imagination or a wisp of cloud, they blew away into the aether, never to be heard from again.

However, as the 19th century gave way to the 20th, flying vehicles only became more prominent. Humanity entered the clouds with the invention of the airplane, which heralded a new century of air commerce, where eventually, we could travel around the world, literally from one end to the other, in little more than a day.

Yet, despite all the advances that came with such an invention, there came downsides also. Not just downsides either, but outright horrors.

Flight may have brought us together, but it only increased our capacity for mass death. The two world wars that followed within fifty years of those airships were the most devastating conflicts in human history. The second one, in particular, featured carnage unlike any we could have imagined.

It just so happened to end when a plane dropped two atomic weapons on Japan.

Just what, then, was the meaning of those airships? Were they glimpses into the future? In the cases we have been examining thus far, there have been suggestions that perhaps the pilots of these strange vehicles come to Earth to provide us with technology. Perhaps, as some people say, they spur us on to become a more advanced civilization, gifting us with wheels and teaching us agriculture. If they can do that, can they not also show us the future of air travel?

Whatever the case, the appearance of these airships no doubt precedes the century that would come to rely on air travel more and more. They appear to us as a kind of bookend or perhaps even a foreshadowing.

The century of industrialization looks to the skies and sees its own future coming to them from the clouds. Maybe these visions were a lesson. Maybe it was a way for the gods to give us fire one more time.

But then again, as we are about to see, maybe Prometheus overshot his mark once again. Because as we joined the future and left solid ground behind, those strange vehicles in the skies did not just continue.

If anything, they only became more frequent.

Chapter 4:

The Foo Fighters of World War II—Allies and Axis Encounters

The 20th century witnessed what was almost a total reversal of the human experience up until then. It was, in effect, a hundred years' worth of upheaval, with everything from two world wars to the horrors of communism, to the Cold War, to the constant, penetrating terror that came with the promise of nuclear annihilation. Gone were the steampunk daydreams of the Victorians—in were the visions of what we understand now as science fiction, with its emphasis on rocket technology, space exploration, the colonization of other worlds, and monstrous creatures from the depths of our worst nightmares.

The moment that the second half of the century hinged upon was, of course, World War II. It was—and remains—the most dramatic period in human history when the fate of the world really was at stake. Fortunately for all of us, the fascist triplets in the form of Japan, Italy, and Nazi Germany all came up short in their efforts to dominate the world stage. But in order to get there, tens of millions of lives were lost, and technologies were developed that would leave history reeling from their effects.

The most famous among those technologies is, of course, the atomic bomb. But before it was developed by the Manhattan Project and subsequently dropped on Nagasaki and Hiroshima, thereby ending the Second World War conclusively, other, more modest technologies were developed that brought havoc and death upon the chilly climes of Europe.

Of these, we may think of tanks, flamethrowers, and other weapons of terrestrial warfare. Certainly, these were instrumental in deciding the fate of the armies involved, and tanks, in particular, continue to be an integral part of modern war. We might also think of the enormous battleships, with their titanic cannons blasting at each other from the Pacific all the way to the Mediterranean.

However, WWII also saw the airplane used as an instrument of war, and to an extent, that would not have been possible at any other time previously. Sure, they had some limited use in the Great War. But WWII was the era of the dogfight, of the ace fighter pilot. It was the time when fast-moving aircraft chased each other through the skies, performing wild, dramatic maneuvers, only to come crashing to the earth after performing that long, musical whine, steadily growing in pitch until it smacked straight into the land below.

For the first time, a human being could travel through the clouds using an invention of his own design. He could fight for the future of civilization from an angle that could only be dreamed of until then, as men imagined themselves as birds or gods, finally overcoming the cruel grasp of gravity.

He had conquered the skies. But when he got up there, he found that something had already beaten him to the punch.

Something in the heavens had been waiting for him.

Strange Things Over European Skies

Early in the morning on September 6, 1943, the U.S. First and Third Bombardment divisions were to lead an attack on Stuttgart, Germany (Chester, 2007). Stuttgart was an industrial city and of great importance to the German war effort. Taking this city's factories out would deal a heavy blow to Hitler, and so the Bombardment divisions—comprising well over 600 airplanes—were assigned the task of blowing it all to hell.

Being a city of importance to the war meant it was well-defended, however. The crewmen were advised that they would meet with heavy resistance, likely in the form of what they called "flak," meaning anti-aircraft shells.

This was precisely what happened. The Americans were hit with an incredible amount of artillery, which erupted around them just as the Nazi air force, the Luftwaffe, took flight. This led to an epic battle in the skies, leading quite literally to thousands of deaths.

But amid all this chaos, something remarkable happened.

At least two of the crewmen during the air raid stated that they had seen "silvery discs" about the size of a silver dollar. These strange objects floated downward as if from something that had broken into pieces above them. But while they were initially assumed to have been from flak, this turned out not to be the case.

Indeed, as news of the silvery discs spread, more and more pilots encountered what could only be described as "swarms" of them. Some of these swarms were up to 75 feet long and 25 feet wide. Pilots who flew under or through the clusters claimed that they could hear the discs pelt the outside of their planes, determining that they were of solid mass.

But what made the reports especially concerning was that these discs seemed to burn the planes they made contact with. Several pilots stated that they may have been made of thermite or something else that ignited similarly. But whatever it was made of, the concern quickly spread that the Nazis had a new and dangerous weapon of war.

That was not all, either. As the Allies began investigating these reports, there were others that came in that seemed to describe further encounters with flying objects that could perform strange maneuvers. The worry of course was that the Axis powers had made a secret leap forward in their technological capabilities, and that the Allies would have to discover the root of this and reverse engineer it in order to not get ahead.

Some of these reports were, no doubt, quite concerning. In addition to the flammable silvery discs, there were worries that the Nazis had remote control bombs. Some information on the silvery discs seemed to indicate that they were coming either from German planes or from somewhere even further above those planes.

It was during this time that a familiar shape—familiar to us, anyway—was reportedly seen by Allied aircraft. Many of these pilots said that they saw things flying through the skies that were shaped like pie plates and silvery in color. It was a shape that we might think of as a kind of saucer. Some of these would streak across the sky at unbelievable speeds, so quickly that their details could not be made out.

The pilots at the time did not know what to make of these things. They were kids, most of them, and were witnesses to carnage beyond what was ever thought possible. The air force was subject to a high casualty rate, and the German rockets were so frightening that many of these pilots would have been in a constant state of terror. There is no doubt that the level of anxiety would make aerial phenomena confusing on a good day, so it cannot be ruled out that the pilots were misinterpreting sensory data. However, reports continued to come in from all corners that these were things one could encounter in the sky, which made it an area of international concern.

These sightings were recorded by British and American Air Force personnel and placed in a file labeled "Phenomena." Some of the men who filed these reports would claim that photo negatives existed of the flying saucers but that these were edited out for official presentations. But even the average Air Force desk jockey had to admit, whether these were hallucinations brought on by stress or not, that something terrifying was happening around those pilots.

It is in this environment that we first encounter what came to be known as the foo fighters.

Foo Fighters: Terror In The Clouds

In the august years of the war, when Germany was launching its last big counteroffensive in Belgium, General Omar Bradley received a memo titled "SECRET PRIORITY" (Chester, 2007). The memo described a strange event just prior to a savage artillery barrage by the Germans, which was thought significant enough to warrant General Bradley's attention.

What the memo described was this: On December 13, sometime just before midnight, radar picked up two signals, identified as aircraft, but making odd maneuvers. The Americans shot at these two objects with artillery and hit them both. The first one "disintegrated," and the second one crashed. The next night, radar picked up more objects, traveling about 100 mph (slow for aircraft) and at an altitude of about a thousand yards. Once more, when they were shot with artillery, they "disintegrated."

The memo specified that these vehicles—if that was indeed what they were—made no sound. In fact, by "disintegrated," the memo meant that there was no sound *when they were hit with artillery either.* Meaning that these crafts did not explode.

In the same area, more events like this were reported by military personnel. This led to several pilots and infantrymen noticing "lights in the sky," some of which appeared to be following them in a T-formation. They were encountered simultaneously across western Europe, in France, Belgium, and the German border.

Eventually, the soldiers decided it might be best to name the lights. They settled on "Foo Fighters," which was inspired by a favorite comic strip, Smokey Stover. The name stuck, and that is what they are known as to this day.

The sightings continued from there. Case after case was filed, leading to the army's conclusion to address the phenomenon. It did so only by proclaiming it a "mystery," but there was enough talk about these mysterious flying objects that they felt it should have been addressed in some manner.

Pilots reported being chased by foo fighters that could change color and glow. Foo fighters appeared during airborne battles over Belgium. Two men pursued one, thinking it was a German plane, until they realized the object left no contrail and did not show up on radar. Those two men were unable to attack the object, which they quickly realized was triangular-shaped and possibly three lights. That chase lasted five minutes until the foo fighter(s) departed.

As was the case with the silver discs, the Allies became concerned that the Germans had developed a new type of weapon. Since the Nazis had been pushed back into their own territory, they would be getting desperate, perhaps leading them to invoke terrible technological forces in order to gain control of the war. One theory was that the foo fighters were robot projectiles.

In response, the British and American Air Forces sent pilots out to try and encounter the foo fighters on purpose. At least two patrols did, in fact, find foo fighters and reported that they, the foo fighters, had behaved in much the same way as had been reported: strange lights that did not show up on the radar, which pursued the Allied pilots until they disappeared.

By then, the existence of the foo fighters was a kind of legend amongst the pilots, and many of them were scared. What if the Germans really did have some advanced weapon? The skies were filled with death as it was—the last thing those boys needed was something else to keep them up at night.

This led Major Augspurger of the Air Force to take his own plane into the skies, hoping to gain information on what these things were and perhaps put his men's fears to rest. He went up in his plane, a fearsome thing with a stallion painted on the nose, and went hunting for foo fighters.

After a long night of searching, he finally found one: a white light that flew parallel to him but did not show up on the radar. Four to five minutes passed as Augspurger tried to get a sense of the object before the white light shot straight up into the sky at a tremendous speed.

After the Major landed, he filed a report with the General and compared his notes with the other sightings they had on record. Between them, they determined that this could not have been a flare or any other projectile. It must have been something technological—except for the fact that they could not explain how it had behaved in the way that it had.

Whatever it was, it was beyond the capabilities of anything either of them had ever heard of. Which meant that neither of them had any idea what the foo fighters could have been.

Meanwhile, one of the RAF's ace interrogators, a man named S.D. Felkin compiled a document of interviews with German prisoners, in which they were specifically asked about "jet-propelled aircraft" being used at night (Chester, 2007). Oddly, the Germans ridiculed the suggestion that they had been using such a thing but said that they had also seen similar phenomena, particularly that of mysterious flying objects.

The foo fighters, or whatever they were, were not only being seen by American and British pilots—meaning, this was no German superweapon. Something else was going on here.

One of the major turning points in this narrative was to come on New Year's Eve, 1944. A reporter for the Associated Press named Bob Wilson arrived at an air force base in France with the intention of writing what would have been quite the puff piece: He intended to join a flight crew that night and describe for the people at home what it was like to fly over war-torn Europe at the beginning of the new year, 1945.

However, weather conditions were quite terrible, and Wilson's guides were forced to land. His story came to nothing. But as he was grounded at the Air Force base, he got to spend some time with the men there and listened to their stories. As he did, he began to piece together that something remarkable was happening in the skies.

Once Wilson had enough for a story, he was able to sell it to several papers, including the *New York Times*. Soon enough, it spread all over America, printing the accounts of pilots, officers, and others who had had an encounter with these mysterious lights in the sky. Many of them described suspenseful chases through the air as pilots tried to outmaneuver these glowing lights that insisted on following them at great lengths, causing horror amongst the crewmen being pursued.

As the story hit the press, it came, too, with a number of possible explanations. Many of these theories took it for granted that the foo fighters were themselves real, technological, and employed by the Nazis. The only question was what precisely they were *doing*.

One theory said that they may have been intended as a kind of psychological warfare designed specifically to distress the pilots. Another said they may have acted as location finders for anti-aircraft guns, allowing the batteries to find their target much more easily. (Regarding the distance the foo fighters kept between them and their objects, it was suggested that perhaps the distance could be compensated for via searchlight. Otherwise, aiming straight for the foo fighters themselves would result not in hitting an Allied plane but a significant piece of German technology.)

But the "soundest" explanation, it was said, was the following: The metal in the planes must have been activating some sort of a gas, which was attracted to the plane magnetically and followed the plane around at a constant distance, until whatever process that created the magnetism wore itself out. This was said to explain how it was that the foo fighters remained at a seemingly consistent distance, even at 200 mph, before retreating.

Soon enough, the story became something of a sensation. This led to a kind of epidemic of lay scientists attempting to explain away the phenomenon. Mostly, they used variations of "St Elmo's fire, but different," or even ball lightning, to settle the debate once and for all—but for every explanation, there seemed to be someone else with one they claimed to fit the facts even better.

The flurry of confusion, as evidenced by the sheer variety of possible explanations, eventually led to an official inquiry. Hitler was near to the point of giving up, and the military naturally wanted to get a hold of this strange technology he was using in the latter, more desperate days of the war.

In fact, the going theory remained that the Nazis had developed a variety of secret superweapons and that this was what the air force was coming up against. One official document at the time, listing the weapons used by the German adversary, had a section titled "Other Weapons," which dealt with "actual or potential weapons" that were or may have been, in use but which were novel enough to be relegated to a kind of miscellaneous category.

In this section, the silver spheres from earlier made an appearance, although their ultimate source was still a mystery. But here, the document mentioned "PHOO" bombs as magnetic devices that seemed to possess, it was said, no real threat to anybody.

Whatever the case, sightings continued into 1945, and worries about their capabilities continued. Further foo fighters were spotted in the Pacific theater (Chester, 2007, chapter 12), which only added further mystery and deepened interest in the subject. But even as investigations trudged forward, nobody seemed able to settle on an answer regarding just what these things were.

Once the Germans were defeated, there was a theory among some investigators that suddenly having access to Germany's files would provide the answer they were looking for (Chester, 2007, chapter 18). There were literal tons of documents at the Allies' disposal, many of which were regarding aeronautical research. If there was anything that would finally give the Allies the information they sought on the foo fighters, these files would be just that thing.

Yet, that information was nowhere to be found. Certainly, there was plenty of confidential information now in the hands of the Americans and the British. A diligent effort was made to uncover the nature of the foo fighters, if for no other reason than to finally put an end to speculation. However, at no point in their extensive research did any of the investigators put in charge of reading these documents find anything that pointed to the existence of the foo fighters.

Even after all that, after putting an end to the Nazi menace and all those hours of poking and prodding, they were nowhere closer to learning the truth.

The Mystery In The Pacific

As previously mentioned, while the war raged on at its peak, there were reports of foo fighters not just over Europe but in the Pacific.

By 1945, the fight against Imperial Japan continued in the form of an extensive bombing campaign (Chester, 2007, chapter 19). Japan resisted with fierce opposition, all the while pursuing a dream of secret weapons—a dream we now know included attempts at making an atomic bomb. While the specifics of their secret weapons program were not known to the Allies at the time, it was nonetheless known that Japan was interested in making a weapon of genuine horror, which no doubt led to increased terror on the part of the American soldiers.

When they, the American air force in Japan, saw foo fighters for themselves, then, it must have been an experience beyond comprehension.

Air intelligence at the time indicated that they had seen what may have been flares or rockets but which were behaving strangely. Much like what happened in Europe, the speculation revolved around the possibility of novel weapons developed by Imperial Japan, including remote-controlled warheads. There was even enough information on the types of lights seen and the formations they were seen in for intelligence to develop a classification system, calling them "Illuminating Flares," "Rocket Projectiles," or "Midget Aircraft" (Chester, 2007, chapter 19).

Combat personnel were encouraged to report these sightings as worries mounted. As the war lurched closer and closer to its conclusion, more reports of "balls of fire" came in, many describing these objects as chasing pilots down at a high speed and requiring evasive maneuvers to get away from.

The sheer number of sightings is almost mind-boggling. Pilot after pilot, intelligence officers, everyone seemed to encounter one of these things. Still, the theory that these were secret weapons prevailed, causing an unbelievable amount of fear among the Allied participants in that war.

But if, at the end of the war in Europe, the hope was that finally, information regarding these things would become available, that hope—if the war against Japan ended in an American victory—was even stronger this time. The mystery had only deepened, and the urge to get an answer was only that much stronger.

But is that what happened?

The Answers

We all know how and when the war ended. The United States Air Force dropped a pair of the scariest weapons ever devised on the Japanese cities of Nagasaki and Hiroshima, and Japan surrendered almost immediately.

Since then, Japan has gone on to become a staunch ally of the United States and one of the most prosperous countries in the world. Like Italy and Germany, it has managed to distance itself from the brutality of its experiments with fascism, and become a beacon of peace and liberty.

But what of its secret aeronautic technology? Did they have weapons capabilities unknown to the Allies at the time? Was there an answer to just what the foo fighters were hiding somewhere in their documents, which had become available as a result of the end of the war?

Unfortunately, no. To date, *there has never been an explanation as to what happened* (chapter 22). Despite all the manpower and all the man-hours put into digging through documents, nobody has ever conclusively determined what a foo fighter was. They have never learned what the silver objects that fell from the skies were either. But no matter their wish, that they could scratch this itch, that they could find a plan for some type of air vehicle that could make those maneuvers, that made no sound, and that did not show up on radar—they found no such plan.

The reason they did not find such a plan was because none of the Axis powers had one. Whatever the foo fighters were, they were not a device that was made or used by any of the fascist militaries.

A War Between Men—and Something Else

The traditional picture of any war is as a war between factions of, generally, men, engaged in a type of mass slaughter in order to accomplish a set of goals. In the Second World War, the fight was between a group of Western liberal democracies, along with their temporary Soviet allies, and the fascist, imperialist countries, who had been caught up in a fanatical fever and developed a desire for world domination.

But what if that was not the whole story?

From our own studies here, it seems as though there was another participant in this war as well. This participant appeared to use technology at a level beyond the understanding of even the most dedicated investigators. It wrought havoc upon the emotional states of young pilots, themselves already in the grip of delirium caused by their experiences with mass death. They emerged from places unknown, for reasons unknown, to perform tasks unknown.

Whatever the truth of the matter, it was clearly the beginning of something. Because for the next almost 100 years, similar, if not identical, phenomena have been reported all across the globe.

But if this was the prologue, the first chapter was to begin with something of a bang—a *crash*, if you will—and take us to the sleepy deserts of New Mexico, where a single event would incite a global phenomenon.

Chapter 5:

Roswell and the Rise of Modern UFOlogy

Back in the 1960s, Philip J. Corso was a lieutenant colonel who studied Foreign Technology at the Pentagon (Corso and Birnes, 1998). He was involved in a wide variety of projects that involved sniffing out Kremlin double agents working in the U.S. government, as well as trying to free captured American soldiers who, after the Second World War, had been thrown into the Soviet gulag system.

But there was one filing cabinet in the Pentagon offices that housed some of the biggest secrets in government history. That cabinet contained what was known as the *Roswell files* and told the story of what the Army pulled from the crashed disc in the deserts of New Mexico.

At some point, due to the demands of his job, Philip Corso familiarized himself with the contents of those files. As an intelligence officer, this should not be surprising. But what he found in there was to shock and disturb him to such an extent that as he entered the twilight years of his life, he decided to publish a book about it.

It is that book which we will concern ourselves with here.

Is his account trustworthy? This is the question that has been asked about this book since its publication in 1998. However, while the claims it makes will test the credulity of anyone willing to explore them, nobody has ever proven that Colonel Corso was engaged in deception. Nobody has shown him to be delusional, a grifter, or to possess any other quality that would make us question his credibility.

Instead, Colonel Corso was a man who spent his years serving his country. His credentials have never been disputed, and in his book, he records then-Senator Storm Thurmond vouching for him as a man to whom we should give our attention (Corso and Birnes, 1998). In other words, he appears to be of impeccable character.

How this affects your interpretation of what is to follow, we will leave up to you. But as we are concerning ourselves with his version of the events, it is important that we state upfront that we see no reason to doubt the story he told. Indeed, the story he told appears to be horrifyingly true.

This is the story of the UFO crash in Roswell, New Mexico. Of the strange and terrifying implications for us and our world.

The Crash

In the weeks preceding the crash, there were hints that something was amiss.

For several days, Army radar picked up strange blips around their nuclear and missile testing sites (Corso and Birnes, 1998). The blips themselves appeared to possess a kind of freedom unknown to aircraft at the time—indeed, it appeared as though these aircraft could move from one end of the sky to the next, with very little time elapsing between destinations.

This put the military on high alert. They sent scout ships out to get a visual on what these things were, but pilots reported no sightings despite the persistence of these blips. Even so, base commanders were clear that the mere presence of these blips, and the fact of their hovering around nuclear testing facilities, indicated a hostile "something" was in the area.

Meanwhile, several residents reportedly saw strange lights in the sky. Given that this was early July, many of them wrote these sightings off as being either lightning or some preparatory fireworks for Independence Day. In fact, nobody seemed to think that any of these phenomena could indicate the presence of flying saucers.

But for military intelligence, things were getting more and more tense. The blips continued with such an astonishing regularity that Army Counter Intelligence became involved. They sent undercover men and women out into the open to try and weed out who the likely Soviet agents were and learn what type of device they were using to spy on the test site.

But then, before they could learn anything through these methods, something crashed.

The military scrambled to reach the crash site. An entire convoy rushed through the desert to find the object, composed of military police, engineers, and intelligence personnel. Fortunately, the object was not difficult to find, as it had already been spotted by a pair of Indian hunters, who reported the location to the authorities.

When they arrived, however, they found something much different than they had been expecting. Many of the men were veterans of World War II, and so they were accustomed to seeing downed planes. This, however, was no downed plane.

What was immediately obvious was that this craft—if that was what it was—was shaped more like a saucer. It had a pair of fins on the top sides and a split seam that ran down the middle. Even after several hours of being stuck in the ground, the craft was still sizzling.

The weirdest part, however, came from a man named Steve Arnold. According to Corso's book, Steve Arnold, who had previously been posted to Roswell's airfield control tower, arrived on the scene and approached the crashed object. As he did, a group of medics gained entry into the ship to look for the wounded.

One of them said three of the most haunting words one can possibly imagine: "*Are those people?*"

At least, until one of the other medics responded with: "*Jesus, I think this one's alive.*"

At this, Steve Arnold turned and found the second medic crouched over a humanoid creature that lay in the sand. This creature appeared to be in agony. It shuddered and made a sound that Arnold said appeared not to come from the creature's mouth, but from its *mind.*

Arnold watched with an overwhelming sadness as the creature struggled to breathe and propped itself up as if to stand. One of the soldiers nearby, no doubt terrified at the sight, screamed, "Halt!" and raised his rifle.

Someone tried to stop this soldier, but not in time. The soldier fired a volley of shots into the creature and killed it instantly.

From there, the soldiers got to work collecting the creatures, as well as their craft. They were able to get the craft onto a flatbed, although not before the contents were seen by several military personnel.

Every one of them was told to stay quiet about this. "Strictly military business," was how one officer put it. Some of them no doubt complied with the order. Several of them told their story to Colonel Corso after he was tasked with interviewing them many years later.

The crash that landed in the consciousness of every American in the years since then had happened. But for Corso, that was not the end. In fact, even greater horrors were about to come.

EBE

The U.S. government suddenly found itself in the possession of an advanced technology, far beyond anything human beings were—and are—capable of. That this occurred during the Cold War was no doubt seen as quite the boon by those involved.

But more than that, perhaps, they had the body of more than one alien life form—an EBE or extraterrestrial biological entity. These specimens, they reasoned, may contain the secrets for long-distance space travel that humanity so desperately craved.

According to Corso, who was familiar with the creature's medical records, it possessed a large heart, which would have allowed it to pump blood through its body using fewer beats per second (Corso and Birnes, 1998). This heart, however, was quite decayed by the time it reached the medical examiner, suggesting that our atmosphere was quite toxic to it.

Meanwhile, its "blood" was a milky substance that passed through a kind of reduced capacity circulatory system. This suggested to the medical examiner that perhaps these creatures had a much longer biological clock than humans. Maybe long trips through space were not as taxing to them, because of the sheer length of their lifespans.

Further deductions suggested that the crashed ship was a scout ship of some kind, possibly one that could refract light to give the illusion of invisibility. If this were true, then perhaps the aliens were never intended to leave the ship, hence why they were so woefully unprotected from Earth's toxic atmosphere.

What interested the medical examiners the most, however, was that these creatures were humanoid. In a way, this was incongruous with our expectations of extraterrestrial life. Science fiction had imagined all manner of bizarre creatures, from reptilians to enormous insects, to, in the case of Lovecraft, beings beyond our ability to make sense of.

But here were beings from another planet who were, instead, quite a lot like us. How could this be? The reason we resonated so much with the insects and reptilians in science fiction magazines may have been because these are the only creatures on Earth who feel truly alien to us. Yet the symbolic value of these fictions was not lost on anybody. We expected "alien" to be the operative word when it came to the biology of alien life forms.

Questions about evolution were bound to arise in a situation like that. Was there something about being a humanoid that made you suited to navigating terrestrial space, no matter the particulars? Certainly, on our world, there are few places we cannot navigate, except where extreme temperatures are present. Could this be a literal *universal*—something that holds in virtually every environment throughout the stars?

But while the presence of this alien corpse suggested mysteries on a much larger scale, the body itself was something of a puzzle. There were further questions about how these things took in energy and expelled waste, especially since the craft seemed to have no method of food preparation or storage (Corso and Birnes, 1998). While the doctors determined that the aliens were made of elements familiar to us, they were nonetheless puzzled as to whether these were carbon-based life forms or something else.

All of this, however, pales in comparison with the facts of the creature's brain.

Here, we should return to Steve Arnold for a moment. He stated that when he saw the creature struggling, it made a screaming sound, but not with its mouth—rather, it made it with its mind. Other witnesses to the crash, too, reported intense feelings of empathy and sadness around it, far beyond what they felt was normal for them. Some of them even said that the creature seemed to communicate a profound mourning for its dead crew mates, as it knew they were all about to die.

If these reports were accurate, then it seemed, at least to the military, that perhaps the creatures were *telepathic.* At the very least, they seemed able to project empathic information to other beings, even if there was no evidence of them being able to communicate complex ideas using the same method.

Regarding the brain itself, the medical examiners said that it was, alas, quite decayed by the time they received it. However, they were nonetheless able to make several observations, all of which are fascinating.

To begin with, while the human skull is quite thick and hard, these creatures' skulls were "soft and spongy" (Corso and Birnes, 1998). The brain itself appeared to be in four hemispheres, or, rather, spheres, and although no hard evidence could be found regarding a portion of the brain that would allow for telepathic communication, it was quite obvious that the brain was, indeed, much larger, and more *alien*, than ours.

In essence, this was a creature that was simultaneously familiar and almost impossibly alien. It suggested mysteries on a scale we had not dreamed of and posed questions that threatened to undermine the totality of our assumptions about who we are and what our place is in the universe.

Intriguing as all that was, however, it was nothing compared to what was discovered about the crashed vehicle.

Technology

One of the central claims in Corso's book is that the government was able to reverse engineer much of the technology aboard that spacecraft. But even more incredibly, that we are surrounded by the fruits of that technology *right at this very second.*

For example, he claims that "fiber optics" were first discovered aboard this alien spaceship (Corso and Birnes, 1998). He says further that the idea of super-compressed fibers came from the same source, but in an interesting twist, also claims that Richard Feynman, who first publicly theorized that such things might be possible, had been in touch with some of the people who had had first-hand experience with the UFO.

Kevlar, too, is supposed to have come from the UFO. A whole host of other everyday objects, too numerous to list here.

Perhaps strangest of all, however, was what appeared to be a headband—a large, metal one that was, he says, worn by the aliens during their travels (Corso and Birnes, 1998).

This headband's function eluded researchers for quite some time. It was adjustable, but only within the range of the aliens' big heads. The human head was, generally, much too small for it to fit snugly around. Some of the men with bigger heads who put the headband on claimed that it gave them quite a shock.

What researchers eventually figured out, however, was that it was both a means of piloting the ship, as well as a means for turning the pilot into a kind of battery. In other words, the body's electrical energy would help power the ship.

Now that the purpose of this technology has been determined, Corso says, we can expect to see it implemented in all sorts of ways. He suggests that we look out for this technology in the realm of gaming but also as a means of piloting our own aircraft.

Whether or not that winds up being the case, the argument he makes in this book is that the crashed UFO has had more of an influence on our civilization than might first be apparent. Not only has it provided us with a pseudo-folkloric touchstone (which is not to say that it is not true), it has gifted us technology that exists in the everyday.

But how is it that we could live in a world that was irrevocably altered by this event and yet be told that it did not happen?

What precisely does the government say happened that day—and what does that mean for us, the public?

The Cover-Up: Or the Truth

The official story runs something like this: In 1947, the Soviet Union was still two years away from getting its own atomic bomb. But in the United States, the only country to have used the weapon on another country, the idea that the Soviets *might* develop one was a cause for paranoia (Webster, 2017). This led to a series of experiments to determine whether nuclear testing could be detected from afar in what was known as *Project Mogul.*

The project involved the use of balloons, which had audio equipment trailing along behind them, and which would be sent across the Pacific and over to Russia. These balloons would, in theory, detect the sound of a nuclear explosion, which would indicate to the American government that such tests were occurring behind the Iron Curtain.

The problem was that one of these balloons went off-course and crashed in the desert in New Mexico. How this happened is a bit of a mystery, but the idea was that the balloon, which was a kind of silver color, spread out all over the ground, looking something like a flying saucer. From there, it was found by locals who did not know what to make of it. So they, like many others, assumed it was something much stranger than it actually was.

Adding to this is the strange fact that, in the immediate aftermath, the Army itself said that they had, indeed, found a flying saucer. This then made it into the papers, which were then dispersed all over the country.

Why did they do this? One explanation is that they were embarrassed by Project Mogul. It would have been bad for international relations had they admitted that they were spying on the Russians. Keeping things civil between the two superpowers, especially as the Cold War was showing early signs of development, must have been a significant priority.

Why they took this initial explanation back, then, may have had something to do with the difficulties beset by making such a claim. For example, it would have been one thing to suggest that an experimental aircraft was downed—but as a lie, to suggest that an alien ship had been discovered would require higher levels of maintenance.

In effect, the official story is that Lieutenant Colonel Corso's version of events is simply not true. There was no UFO crash, no aliens discovered at the site, no alien autopsy, no reverse engineering of technology—nothing. These are untruths at best, fabrications at worst. The reality of the event is merely that the Cold War was beginning to take off, and the United States government was experimenting with 1940s technology to see if they could gather intel from inside Russian borders.

Adding to this version of events is the fact that Project Mogul has since been declassified. Anyone can read all about it online, any time they wish. So far as the government is concerned, the case is closed.

Yet, there is at least one sense in which that is demonstrably not true. Because Roswell was not a book unto itself. It was, rather, the first chapter in a much, much larger story. One that continued to involve spies, military personnel, and others in a search for an answer regarding just what the hell was happening with these flying saucers.

The case on Roswell may have been closed officially. But unofficially, it was nothing more than foreshadowing.

Chapter 6:

Project Blue Book—Decoding U.S. Air Force Investigations

As the Cold War grew in intensity, so did UFO sightings. All over the United States, Europe, and Canada, strange things were seen in the skies, doing things nobody thought possible. Paranoia grew, and as it did, so did the number of theories regarding what was up there.

Russians. Chinese. The CIA.

Aliens.

In response, the government put their best men to the task. As they put it, their job was to provide the public with their discoveries and to withhold nothing. In practice, however, the result was often quite different.

Or so the story says.

This is the story of Project Blue Book—what it was, how long it lasted, and which methods it used. It is a story about a clandestine operation in which high-ranking government officials engaged in a very Cold War-style, domestic version of realpolitik. It is a story about people encountering forces much larger than themselves, whether in the form of the U.S. government or something *else*.

But most of all, it is a story which will leave us, as always, with more questions than answers.

So, just what was Project Blue Book? And what, if anything, did it uncover?

Prehistory

Before Project Blue Book, there was Project Sign. But before Project Sign, there was a man named Kenneth Arnold.

Kenneth Arnold was a pilot. On June 24, 1947, he took his personal plane from the Chehalis, Washington airport, with the intention of flying to Yakima (Steiger, 2019). As he tells it, the air was fine and smooth enough for him to level the plane out, sit back, and enjoy the flight. The sky was clear also, which made for a relaxing atmosphere.

However, a few minutes into his course, a bright light shocked him. He looked around for its source, worried about what might be happening in the skies around him. While he could not find its exact source, he did see something *else* come behind him.

Nine peculiar objects, flying at about 4,500 ft.

"Peculiar," because, while Arnold assumed they were jet aircrafts, they had no tails. They moved rapidly from north to south. They were approaching him at incredible speed. Eventually, they ripped past him, doing over 1,600 mph.

When he was interviewed later, he said that the objects looked like "saucers skipping on water." This was changed by the press to "flying saucers," which gave us our common name for them. But while that was his story, the Air Force was not so sure.

To them, it was clear that Arnold had seen a mirage. The conditions he described could have led to a type of light refraction that can give impressions like those he had. It was just an odd thing that can happen to pilots sometimes.

Arnold, however, was not so sure. He made drawings of the objects and described what he thought was not only their speed, but their dimensions. He remained convinced that he had seen something very real, and that this was not a hallucination, a mirage, or any other type of sensory mishap.

Whatever the truth of the matter, Kenneth Arnold's sighting became the prototypical one. Not long after his encounter was released through the press, the Roswell incident happened, and Americans developed a craze for all things UFO-related.

In response to this rash of sightings, the government started what was known as Project Sign (Ruppelt, 2023). This project was considered to be important enough that only the top people at the Air Technical Intelligence Center (ATIC) were assigned to it—meaning, if you were one of the top spooks, you were in, and nobody else was allowed near. Its task was to receive reports on UFO sightings from around the world, if possible, and try to determine their cause, origin, and whatever else they could about them.

With this objective in mind, Project Sign found itself on the receiving end of some bizarre stories indeed. These included what appeared to be "smudges" in the sky, as well as stories about "ghost rockets" and other things.

Perhaps most memorably, they investigated a report about a dogfight between an F-51 and a UFO over Fargo, North Dakota (Ruppelt, 2023). This event was corroborated by four witnesses and resulted in the human pilot's plane becoming radioactive.

Then, in 1949, Project Sign changed its name to Project Grudge (Ruppelt, 2023). This led to no discernible change in the project's operations, but it was apparently clear by then that the goal of investigating these sightings was to investigate things that could not possibly be real. Meaning that the project's principles were not that UFOs were spaceships piloted by aliens, but something else, and that this was to be the underlying assumption during the investigations.

At some point, this led to Project Grudge becoming the de facto debunking agency. To pull this off, however, would require a two-pronged (or two-phase) solution: In the first, it explained to the public what it had uncovered about the sightings. In the second, which came after the first phase had ended, the project assured everyone that the Air Force had, in fact, solved *all* of the sightings and would then explain how it had done this. This was executed with the hope that doing so could put an end to all these UFO reports.

The first phase had its origins in the Project Sign period and came about because, frankly, most of the UFO sightings were utter garbage. The highest-level intelligence personnel in the US government would find themselves investigating a claim that bizarre, flying crafts had made their way behind American borders, only to find out that the craft in question was nothing more than a hot air balloon. To prevent wasting their own time, they had to find some way to get ahead of the bunk claims so they could spend their time worrying about sightings of significance.

They tried several different ways of pulling this off, but most commonly they tried to speak with reporters, tell them their (the government's) version of what had happened, and then hope this information would clear everything up. The problem, however, was that reporters had a difficult time believing that all of these sightings could be explained as hoaxes, hallucinations, or lies, and said as much in their work.

Finally, however, they found their man, Sidney Shallet, at the *Saturday Evening Post.*

Shallet's work is significant in the history of UFOlogy. While the public was interested in UFOs and had varying degrees of confidence in the extraterrestrial explanation, Shallet's writing had a significant effect in turning public opinion toward skepticism. How he did this was, no doubt, through the power of his writing. But the story goes that he was either told to play down the UFO angle in his articles or else simply wrote whatever it was that Project Grudge told him to write.

In any case, the first phase of Project Grudge's crusade against UFO sightings was in full swing—they could release to the public any and all information about the origins of these sightings, put them at ease, and get on, eventually, with phase two.

But by that time, phase two was quite easy to pull off. Project Grudge needed to scale down its operations in order to make the best use of its time. After debunking thousands of cases and finding the same explanations for all of them, Project Grudge personnel merely said that investigating further sightings would lead to the same conclusions. Basically, they had already gathered the information they needed, and the conclusions were clear. Why bother to continue at the level they had been at before?

In fact, the end result was that Project Grudge folded. The members submitted what was called the Grudge Report, and that was that. The mystery of flying saucers was solved, making Project Grudge a waste of money. Everyone involved went back to their regular jobs in intelligence, and that was that.

At least, for a while.

History

Project Grudge closed up shop on the assumption that UFO sightings would continue but that they had been so adequately explained that they did not need to be the government's problem anymore. Individuals could gather in research groups, write books, and do whatever they wanted with regard to UFOs. But as far as the government was concerned, it was none of their business.

The problem was that civilians were not the only ones who saw UFOs. The Air Force especially kept running into them, which posed something of a problem for ATIC. What were they supposed to do about the fact that their own pilots and their own radar technicians kept reporting sightings of advanced aircraft?

The answer was to resurrect Project Grudge. Only this time, it went by the name of Project Blue Book.

The name was not the only change either. Cognizant of the fact that a significant number (as much as 60%) of UFO sightings are of balloons, Blue Book decided to develop a system to weed out this type of case and instead concentrate on the actual unknowns (Ruppelt, 2023). To do this, they simply kept a record of skyhook balloon flights and would pick up the phone and call the relevant people to get information on research balloons and things of that sort.

They also subscribed to a newspaper clipping service, which allowed them to monitor not just potential UFO sightings, but also public opinion related to UFOs. They also made sure to get constant updates on the weather all over the country, in case a UFO could be explained by an effect of climate.

All this together, and still, there were cases that could not be readily explained. These cases were labeled "Unknown," and some of them wound up explained by further natural phenomena (ducks, apparently, were often mistaken for spaceships.) But once those were dealt with, there were, finally, cases that merited further attention.

The best of these reports were ones that would merit a "boots on the ground" visit. Many of the others would be dealt with by people in the office—which amounted to something like a dozen people—but if they were especially interesting, a field officer would be sent to investigate. But enough of these reports—some 22% of them—that came in were interesting enough to warrant looking into.

From there, Project Blue Book looked into some of the most famous UFO cases in American history. One of these involved an incident where a UFO "buzzed" the White House (Ruppelt, 2023), and which preceded the Project learning that, in fact, DC was often abuzz with UFO traffic. More than once, a fighter jet went in hot pursuit, only to lose the target at the last moment.

One of the more remarkable ones happened to a scoutmaster who was driving his troop of scouts home late at night. The scoutmaster, in his version of the events, was driving past the woods when he saw what looked like a sudden flash of light from behind the trees (Ruppelt, 2023). This bothered him, as he wondered if maybe someone had crashed, and he would have hated it if he had seen something and done nothing about it.

He pulled over and put on a 15-minute radio program. He told the boys in his car that if he was not back by the time the program ended, he should run to the nearest house and call for help. There were rattlesnakes out at night in those woods, and he was going in with little in the way of defense.

He walked about 50 yards into the woods, flashlight in hand, until he found himself in the presence of a strong odor. Not only that, but the temperature suddenly got hotter.

He stepped into a clearing and both the odor and temperature became even more noticeable. This was soon coupled with a terrible sensation of being watched, which was strong enough to make him stop.

At that point, he wondered if he had lost his bearings and so looked up. But he could not see anything—the sky was completely black and devoid of any stars at all. Thinking he was maybe under a canopy, the scoutmaster shone his light up, only to find himself looking at a large, black object.

The sensation of being watched overwhelmed him. At first, he was horrified, but then he became angry. As he said, he wanted to harm the thing that hovered over him if he could find a way to reach it.

Before he could do anything, the shape overhead reacted, almost as if reading his mind. A door opened on its underside, and a fine, red mist poured out, as red as a ball of flame.

The scoutmaster dropped his flashlight and shielded his eyes. The red mist overcame him, and he passed out.

But we should back up here for a second.

At the time that the door on the underside of the object opened, the scouts in the car had a feeling something bad was happening. They ran out into the woods to find the scoutmaster and make sure he was okay.

They came upon him just as he dropped his flashlight. The boys all said they saw him enveloped by what appeared to be a red flame. They saw him pass out, too, at which point they ran to the nearest farm and got help.

The scoutmaster was found, safe but unconscious. He related his story to the farmers who had found him, and then to the police, and finally all the way up the ladder to the men at Project Blue Book.

There were many more cases like this one. The men who worked at Blue Book investigated dozens per day, to total something around 12 thousand cases altogether (Readman, 2024). If the stories they tell are true, then they spent nearly fifteen years in total encountering a world of unknowns, where the difference between science and fiction and reality has broken down.

How the Project ended, however, painted a much different picture of its research.

In 1968, the Project released a report on its findings. This report, called the Condon Report, said that despite the number of unsolved cases (around 700 or so), further research would not yield significant results (Readman, 2024). Since the majority of these cases could be explained by natural phenomena, the report stated that there was no reason for it to continue.

In 1969, the Project was closed down.

Legacy

The idea of government agents investigating the unknown and mysterious has become something of a cultural touchstone in the United States. In our own entertainment media, in fact, we can see its influence, particularly in the realm of television.

One of the most significant shows to use this paradigm was the early '90s hit *Twin Peaks.* In it, Special Agent Dale Cooper of the FBI arrives at the small town of Twin Peaks, Washington, to investigate the murder of a local high school girl. However, once there, he finds himself encountering strange, otherworldly forces, including evil entities that possess the living, and a terrible, parallel dimension known as the Black Lodge.

The show was perhaps at its most influential during its first season. Its second was famously interfered with by studio execs, leading to a reduced quality, as well as reduced interest on the part of its creator, David Lynch. However, its recent third season was a hit, and featured even stranger occurrences, notably doppelgängers and the possibility of time travel.

However, the show most famous for its treatment of government agents galivanting across America in search of the paranormal is undoubtedly *The X-Files.*

That show, which ran for nine seasons, two movies, and then two *more* seasons, featured two FBI agents—one a believer, one a skeptic—who chased down everything from sewer-dwelling parasitic humanoids to werewolves to, yes, aliens and UFOs. The UFO episodes, which told a continuous story separate from the "monster of the week" episodes, involved abductions, government cover-ups, and an experimental program to breed alien-human hybrid super-soldiers.

It was outlandish, to be sure. But it is noticeably drawn from Project Blue Book's well, even down to the epistemological ambiguities the real Project no doubt encountered: *How much of this is real? If real, what are they, and where do they come from? Is something being kept from us?*

To this day, *The X-Files* remains a popular and masterful piece of American popular television. As recent events in UFOlogy have shown, it remains frighteningly relevant.

The Legacy in the Real World

The modern-day Pentagon program that investigates UFOs is called the All-domain Anomaly Resolution Office. It currently serves as a kind of central hub, collecting reports from across the DOD—meaning the Army, Navy, and Air Force (Specktor 2022). This began after a number of high-profile videos were released, notably by Blink-182's Tom DeLonge, of what appeared to be wingless ships making strange maneuvers.

Since then, the Navy has declassified a number of its videos featuring what may be UFOs. Many of these are grainy and therefore difficult to make out much of the detail. A slew of FOI requests has led to the Pentagon declassifying some 1,500 documents on UFOs and alleged abductions. Some of these feature stories about strange radiation burns and unaccounted-for pregnancies.

However, in a turn of events strikingly similar to what happened with Projects Grudge and Blue Book, AARO has so far not found any evidence of alien involvement associated with these videos.

Perhaps it is not continuing the legacy of Project Blue Book merely in purpose and design. Perhaps it is doing so in results as well.

***

Project Blue Book officially closed in 1969 and AARO began in 2022. In between those two years, however, there was not a dearth of UFO encounters. Much like what happened in between Projects Grudge and Blue Book, the phenomenon continued unabated.

In fact, as we are about to see, as the Cold War got more and more heated, so did the number of UFO sightings become more frequent.

No matter the findings of the people at Blue Book, the UFO phenomenon was not going away any time soon.

Chapter 7:

Close Encounters of the Cold War—A Global Perspective

The Cold War was maybe the tensest period in the history of humanity.

If WWII was the time when the fate of the world teetered between freedom and totalitarianism, the Cold War not only revived those issues but added to them the possibility of nuclear war. The two superpowers, the United States and the Soviet Union, stockpiled an enormous number of bombs, each trying to outpace the other with the sheer scale of their arsenal. They also engaged in a number of proxy wars, most notably in

Korea and Vietnam, and they competed for influence through Latin America, Africa, and the Middle East.

All this while the destruction of humanity was only a push of a button away.

It was the kind of scenario only dreamed of in science fiction or superhero comics. The idea that a single decision could annihilate life on Earth was no longer the purview of Lex Luthor but a reality. Men like John F Kennedy, Josef Stalin, and Richard Nixon led their respective superpowers with the knowledge that the fate of the world was in their hands. The barriers between fiction and reality, in other words, were breaking down.

High technology was more and more available to the average person. Humanity became a space-faring species with their trips in orbit and, eventually, to the moon. Meanwhile, science fiction media became more prevalent, particularly in cinemas, but also on television. It was a period of enormous change, of strange new cults, drugs, and high anxiety.

It was also the period which saw maybe the most significant increase in UFO sightings.

But how did UFO activity dovetail with the concerns of the Cold War? How did the superpowers respond to the possibility that the other may have been using alien technology? And what did the scientific community think of it all?

To answer these questions, we are going to look at some of the most dramatic events in American and Russian history. Many of these are not as widely known as some of the major epochal changes during this time—the Vietnam War, for example, or the Civil Rights movement. They are, in many ways, hidden phenomena, shoved into the back of a dark closet to be forgotten about.

But they are dramatic. They *did* change things.

And they did—seemingly—happen.

The Washington National Sightings

The UFO sightings at Washington National are among the most publicized in the history of the subject. They were discussed worldwide and led to demands from London, Ottawa, and Mexico City that the President explain what had happened (Ruppelt, 2023). The event even beat out the Democratic National Convention for headline space.

Like many major UFO events—Roswell included—there were signs much earlier that something was amiss. In this case, it was on July 10, 1952, that a National Airlines crew reported a light much too bright to be coming from a balloon, but too slow to be a meteor. This was reported as the plane flew over Quantico, Virginia, which is commonly known as the location where the FBI is located.

Lights were seen again on July 13 by another plane. But on July 14, a Pan American crew claimed to have seen eight UFOs as they passed over the area, appearing to represent something of an escalation. Further evidence for an escalation came two nights later when a variety of lights were seen over the ocean, this time by a high-ranking civilian scientist and another man.

Because of this, some people in the Air Force speculated that perhaps a powder keg of UFO activity was about to go off. And they were right.

The first wave of sightings occurred over the Washington national airport. These appeared as lights, but radar picked them up also. Jet fighters were sent in to intercept, but were not able to overrun the UFOs, which took off at blinding speeds.

Once the dust was settled, Blue Book became involved, and an investigation began. They quickly ruled out that the lights were caused by planes since no planes had been in the area at that time—and, further, the idea that they could have outrun the jets was not to be taken seriously. Regarding radar, it was thought that perhaps a malfunction had caused the objects to appear on the device. However, an examination of the machine proved that it was in perfect working order.

Something had indeed entered the skies that night at Washington National.

Then, a week later, whatever had shown up came back again. Several lights hovered in the sky, all of which showed up on radar again. Jets flew out to intercept them, only for them to disappear and then reappear. After several maneuvers to contain and get a good sight of them, the lights shot off into space, unknown and unseen.

Again, there were no errors in the equipment that could have accounted for this. Instead, everyone involved said that whatever had been out there, hovering over Washington National, had *really been there.*

Just what precisely it was, however, remained elusive.

The newspapers went crazy over the story. Several of them printed headlines indicating that UFOs had indeed been encountered over the airport and referenced Project Blue Book personnel as experts. This led to a flurry of UFO sightings that had the Pentagon jammed up for some time, and especially to some sensationalist reporting techniques.

For example, Daniel Keyhoe wrote a book titled *Flying Saucers From Outer Space*, in which he mentions one General Samford as sitting behind his desk, wrestling with his conscience (Ruppelt, 2023): Should he tell the "real truth" about UFOs, or will the public go into a panic?

As Ruppelt notes, this is tantamount to Keyhoe suggesting he can read minds. There was no way he could have possibly known what the General, nor anyone else, was thinking at that moment. It was a fabrication, a literary embellishment disguised as reportage.

It does, however, shed light on the mood of reporters over the event. It was a sensational story, possibly in the most vulgar sense—the coverage, therefore, was anything but measured.

But while this was almost certainly one of the most-publicized UFO stories during the Cold War, it does little to enlighten us as to the *why* of the increase in UFO sightings between 1946 and 1989. If UFOs are indeed piloted by extraterrestrial visitors, what might explain their increased interest in us during that period?

Malmstrom AFB

The Air Force base in Malmstrom, Montana, was, in 1967, the home of an extraordinary number of intercontinental ballistic missiles (ICBMs). It was, as a consequence, heavily guarded, and equipped with the latest technology for monitoring the security of these nuclear weapons.

On the evening of March 24, 1967, several witnesses reported a strange red light over the base (Hastings, 2006). But while the light in the sky attracted the attention of the men stationed there, they bore witness to an even more terrifying occurrence: The nuclear weapons began to shut down.

According to 1st Lt. Robert C. Jamison, a directive was given for him and several others to begin the process of restarting the missiles. Furthermore, they were told that in the event of a UFO appearing overhead during this process, they were to remain hidden until the UFO had passed—this, seeming to indicate that the officers in charge were aware of the nature of the phenomenon.

Luckily, Jamison's team was able to restart several of the missiles without any activity. Other teams involved in this process did the same, and eventually, the ICBMs were all returned to working condition.

Immediately after this, says Jamison, the men stationed at Malmstrom were given a debriefing on UFOs that lasted two weeks. Once this was completed, they were "dispatched into the field" (Hastings, 2006).

But this was not the end. Weeks later, another UFO was spotted over the Launch Control Facility, leading to the shutdown of four or five ICBMs. These were also restarted without incident.

An investigation was initiated by the Pentagon, involving Project Blue Book. A large number of personnel at the base were able to testify to the fact of a UFO, as well as the directive to remain vigilant to the UFOs presence. The testimonials themselves were given not just by guards and clerks, but also by officers, including Captain Robert Salas.

According to several people involved in the incident, including Captain Salas, the UFO was the cause of the shutdown. Given that it had appeared prior to the malfunction, and the alleged directives given in response to its appearance, this seemed to many of them a logical conclusion.

Despite this, Blue Book concluded that the shutdown was caused by a technical glitch. There was, understandably, a lack of physical evidence that proved a UFO was responsible, and so without any empirical data to support the claim, Blue Book was keen to dismiss it. However, nobody was able to determine precisely which technical glitch it was that shut the missiles down, meaning this explanation was only given due to a lack of other plausible scenarios.

Complicating matters is the fact that Salas continued to advocate for the UFO theory even after Blue Book and others had dismissed it. If he was correct, perhaps the UFOs had an active interest in the nuclear technology used by the two superpowers.

The question then is: Did similar events occur in the Soviet Union? And how did they handle it?

UFOs in the USSR

Given the tight level of control over information in the Soviet Union, it was challenging not only for the citizens of that empire to gain access to information, but for countries outside the USSR's purview. This was especially true of more sensitive topics, particularly where political and technological matters were concerned.

Since the end of the Cold War, however, much of the Soviet Union's internal documentation has been obtained by NATO countries, leading to the dissemination of certain of these sensitive topics. Because of this, a certain amount of their information regarding UFOs, and encounters with the same, have been made available to researchers.

Among these revelations is the fact that the USSR did indeed possess a wealth of information on the subject. Although discussion of the subject was highly restricted (Platov &

Sokolov 2006), it was nonetheless permissible for scholars to give public presentations on UFOs. These were often popular with the public, although, due to issues of political correctness, scholars were expected to use the term "anomalous phenomena" instead of "UFO."

Regarding the restrictions in place, it cannot be said that they were all necessarily unreasonable either. The Soviet Union was worried that the phenomenon had to do with experimental aircraft, or surveillance technology, and therefore sought to limit discussion to the extent that it might reveal military or intelligence secrets. Anyone who wished to spread information about these occurrences was expected to submit proposals to the state for approval—although this was the case for virtually everything within the USSR.

Of the cases themselves, perhaps the most famous—and one which escaped into international media—is the Petrozavodsk phenomenon.

This event happened on September 20, 1977, when the residents of Petrozavodsk reported anomalous phenomena in the skies: in this case, a bright, luminous sphere that emitted light beams (Platov & Sokolov 2006). A more detailed description might say that it resembled a kind of jellyfish, with strange, tentacular "limbs" surrounding the giant sphere of light. The object was said to hover over the town for 10–12 minutes before it passed over the nearby lake and then disappeared.

This aroused the attention of the Soviet authorities. Witnesses claimed that damage was done to windows and buildings as a result of the intense light beams that came off of the object, and several other incidents like this were reported throughout Eastern Europe, including Helsinki. Something very strange seemed to be going on.

The Soviet Academy of Sciences initiated an investigation, in which they considered a variety of possibilities. These included that the object was the result of atmospheric phenomena, as well as causes related to rocket testing. A satellite had been launched at the time of the incident, and so this was given special consideration.

In fact, it was this satellite, known as Cosmos-955, which was officially declared the cause of the jellyfish-like object. That it may have caused atmospheric disturbances could explain why strange things were seen in the skies over Finland and other Eastern European countries.

However, even as this non-alien explanation was given the rubber stamp, the Soviets understood that the UFO phenomenon was worthy of study. This may have been, at least in part, driven by the possibility that these represented serious violations of national security—at least if the previous patterns regarding American government interest in the same. But whatever the case, the Soviets understood that it was time to develop a program that took this seriously.

Enter the SETKA program.

This was, in some ways, the USSR's answer to Project Blue Book, but with some noticeable differences. What they had in common was that SETKA, too, would investigate possible UFO sightings, as well as collect data from military sources. However, while Blue Book closed shop in 1969, SETKA began in the '70s and lasted until the dissolution of the USSR (Platov & Sokolov, 2006). Combined with the fact that their operations took place under a brutal dictatorship, SETKA was operating under a very different set of circumstances.

All in all, SETKA investigated thousands of possible sightings, although, like Blue Book, it found that the vast majority of them were, in the end, quite natural: weather balloons, planes, and the like were often implicated.

However, by the time the program was disbanded, there were still several hundred cases marked "unidentified" (Platov & Sokolov 2006). These would have to remain as such, as, in 1990, the Soviet Union was at the end of its lifespan. The Soviet government had to frantically reallocate money in order to slow down the effects of its collapse. In the end, this was to be all for naught, and the program, along with the rest of the Soviet tyranny, was ended.

That said, there were several interesting finds during the SETKA period that dovetail with what the Americans learned during the same period. For example, there was some indication that UFOs tended to cluster around areas of military significance: nuclear testing sites, for example, but also testing sites for other technologies (Platov & Sokolov 2006).

This raises the specter, of course, of the possibility that these UFOs really *were* sent by American or Soviet intelligence in order to gather intel. However, given that the Soviets seemed as confused by these technologies as the Americans, this seems unlikely.

Additionally, in cases where UFOs were seen by civilian populations near test sites, it could be that people really were witnessing experimental aircraft or missile technology and mistaking them for something more alien. The case of Cosmos-955 lends some credence to this and would provide a much simpler explanation for why UFOs tended to be seen around military installations.

Whatever the case, the similarities between the cases in both the United States and the Soviet Union are striking. But how did each of these countries view the other's interest in UFOs?

Paranoia and Spying

Even after the end of the Cold War, information on how these two state entities viewed each other's interest in UFOs remains largely speculative.

Some of how they viewed UFOs in relation to one another has been covered by the fact that each appeared to suspect that UFOs were the result of some technological leap in spy technology on the part of the other. The Americans certainly have had a long and storied relationship between encountering strange objects and assuming it was enemy technology.

But how did, say, Reagan view the Soviet interest in UFOs, if he was even aware of it? Would he or his cabinet have seen it as ridiculous? Would they have considered it a ruse? This information is not readily available so far as research for this book has turned up.

Most interesting to wonder about is how this was understood by the Cold War's two great paranoids, Richard Nixon and Josef Stalin. Each was known to be pathologically suspicious of virtually everyone around them. Stalin's paranoia led to more suffering than any one person has ever caused in the history of the world—minus the incompetence and ideological fervor of Chairman Mao. Nixon's paranoia led to the Watergate scandal, which undermined the American public's trust in government to such an extent that it has not since recovered.

Some context here might be of help. Nixon assumed the presidency in 1969, which was the year Project Blue Book said UFOs were not a threat to national security. If he ever received information regarding Soviet UFO sightings, Blue Book's findings would likely have colored his understanding of them. But since Nixon never spoke publicly about UFOs, any thoughts on the subject remain highly speculative.

Regarding Stalin, there is one piece of information that is interesting regarding his feelings toward UFOs. Returning to the year 1947, we find that Western intelligence suspected the USSR of using experimental aircraft over Scandinavia (Anton and Vugrin, 2022), which may or may not have been true. But most fascinating is that while investigating this, they learned that the Soviets had been interested in the UFO as a tool for psychological warfare.

The idea here seems to be that the UFOs can be used to create fear and confusion. Given the terrain covered in this book thus far, there appears to be ample evidence for this idea. In virtually every significant case where a UFO has been spotted, it is accompanied by an extended period of speculation, where the public and the press try to explain the event. Given the sheer number of explanations floated during these periods, this might signal that there is indeed a surplus of confusion following major UFO sightings.

In the case of the Soviet Union, this opens up two possibilities. First, the Soviet Union's reign was marked by roughly a hundred years of terrorizing its own citizens. The idea that they would have considered manufacturing UFO encounters in order to keep the public afraid is not beyond the realm of possibility.

At the same time, is it possible that they thought the UFOs were attempting to create fear and confusion *on behalf of the American government?* In other words, did they perhaps suspect that the Americans were sending UFOs into the Soviet Union for the purposes of psychological warfare?

These are not things we will know. But suffice it to say, as this was a period defined by its paranoia, particularly in its constant suspicion of virtually every person, that the American and Soviet governments not only suspected the other of being behind UFO technology while *perhaps* suspecting that the other may have been up to something with regard to their *interest* in UFOs—this is not unthinkable.

***

The UFO phenomena in the United States and the Soviet Union was both a symptom and a cause of the prevailing emotion during this period—that of paranoia. It is emblematic of everyone's suspicion that the Other was hiding something that there were things beyond the scope of our observation that would only occasionally poke its head out.

Yet, that UFOs clustered around military installations might be no coincidence. If there really are beings out there who visit the Earth in their ships, perhaps there was something about the weapons we built during that time that concerned them. After all, they did at least *appear* to shut down the ICBMs in Montana.

But how to explain this interest? There is no explanation, only speculation. Perhaps they are peaceful and want to discourage us in our efforts to destroy one another. Perhaps they are aggressive and want to cut out our own means of defense.

Then again, maybe all those sightings really were just of experimental aircraft, new weapons technology, and atmospheric phenomena created by satellite launches.

Whatever the case, as the Cold War came to a close, some wrinkles appeared in the notion that UFOs had an express interest in the U.S. and USSR. By the time the '80s arrived, this phenomenon began to take an interest in the European continent, and in a way that put even the most hardened skeptics on their back foot.

Chapter 8:

The Belgian Wave and Europe's UFO Craze

December 11, 1989: Colonel André Amond drove with his wife from their home in Ernage, taking the backroads to meet their son at a nearby train station (Amond et al., n.d.). It was a cold night, right around freezing temperatures. The sky was clear, but it was late and quite dark. Still, the moon was visible alongside the stars.

It was on this drive that he saw a strange sight: three or maybe four of what he called "luminous panels" hovering in the sky. Each of these was trapezoidal, and in the middle was another red light, this one pulsing.

But despite the fact that these lights were clearly separate from each other—since Amond could see the dark spaces between them—they moved in unison. Slowly, they moved, approaching a group of poplar trees.

Amond followed them in his car. He slowed down to stay with them lest he lose them. He watched them move behind the poplars, after which he sped up to get closer and observe whether they emerged from the trees. At that point, he was still entertaining the possibility that he may have been imagining things.

But when he reached the desired location, he learned that he was not imagining things at all. The lights *did* emerge from behind the trees. What is more, his wife saw them too.

Amond parked his car and exited. As he did, he looked up at the moon for a brief moment, then turned to look at the luminous panels. Only now, the panels had changed and become a much different object: a large, circular, white light, which had changed direction. It was now heading straight for Amond and his wife.

Mrs. Amond panicked. She demanded that Amond start the car up, since it appeared the white light was aggressive. Why else would it be coming toward them?

Amond went to enter the car, but as he stood between the door and the body of his vehicle, he looked again at the object. It made no noise—not even an engine sound. It had engaged in a maneuver, which appeared to him strange—it had turned its nose up.

In doing so, the object revealed its ventral side to Amond. It was triangular, with white lights on each of the points and a red light in the middle.

From there, the object rapidly shot off. A train approached. Amond started up the car and left to pick up his son.

The whole incident lasted no more than 10 minutes.

***

This story may sound similar to all the others we have looked at thus far. In fact, it could very well be the case that after reading UFO story after UFO story, the reader has become more or less immune to the sheer strangeness of the details. Certainly, after the EBE autopsy after Roswell, it is challenging to find another peak of quite the same magnitude.

Yet, Colonel and Mrs. Amond's encounter would prove to be one of the more important ones in the history of UFO sightings. Because more than perhaps any other, it is the one that has continued to stump skeptics.

In other words: This one might be the real deal.

But why is that? What is it about this simple UFO sighting in Belgium that has made so many scratch their heads?

What does all of this say about the nature of the phenomenon?

An Inconvenient Truth

The first thing to make mention of is that there were more witnesses than just the Amonds'.

A woman named Huguette Marits was walking along the street, trying to get home from the train station (Amond et al., n.d.). As she tells the story, she saw strange lights behind the nearby poplars. When she got a good look, she saw that the object was a floating equilateral triangle and that there were three lights (yellow, in her telling) on each corner, with a red light in the middle.

The object frightened her. She ran home and told her husband what she had seen. When he looked out to see if anything was still there, he saw nothing. But she remained convinced and even told her closest family and friends.

The question of whether she saw the same object seen by the Amonds is not 100% clear, but there are several reasons to think it probable that she did.

Firstly, it should be said that Marits, who was interviewed about this encounter sometime after the fact, did not remember the exact date. However, when pressed for environmental and atmospheric details, what she remembered corresponded to the Amonds' description of that day. This means that if she was in that area on a day in December when atmospheric details were identical to those the Amonds described, then it is probable she had the encounter on the same day.

If she had that encounter in the same location on the same day, then it is likely she saw the same object. This means that, finally, there were three witnesses to this occurrence, one of whom was entirely independent of the others.

However, the one glaring discrepancy cannot be overlooked: Marits described the lights as yellow, while the Amonds described them as white. This could possibly be explained via the vagaries of memory, as Marits was remembering an incident that occurred years prior, while the Amonds' reported the incident not long after it occurred. Other explanations, such as the closeness of white to yellow under certain atmospheric conditions, might also explain this. However, in the absence of empirical data, they would all be speculative.

The other discrepancy that should be addressed is the Amonds' initial description of the yellow panels. This is how they saw the object initially before seeing it as a triangular object with lights on the underside.

Theoretically, this could be explained by virtue of the angle at which the object was seen. Essentially, if the object was lit underneath by four lights of two colors, perhaps the trapezoidal shapes were lights *on the side of the craft.* They could have been, for example, windows, while the bulk of the craft was obscured by darkness; thus, it would give the appearance of yellow trapezoidal shapes floating one after the other.

This too remains speculative. Perhaps the Amonds had a unique experience that did not line up with the UFO phenomenon, but which is interesting nonetheless. Perhaps it was the case too that Marits' memory had been influenced by something, perhaps something she saw on TV, and what had happened to her was in no way related to what had happened to the Amonds.

Those answers may never become available to us. However, what is known is that this was not the only UFO seen in Belgium during that period.

In fact, more than anything, it was a small part of something much, much stranger.

The Wave

Toward the end of 1989, the Head of Operations of the Belgian Air Staff was a man named Major General Wilfried De Brouwer (De Brouwer, 2010). According to his account, beginning in late November, only a few weeks before the Amonds saw their UFO in the woods, many strange occurrences happened over the quiet Belgian skies.

The first of these occurred on November 29, when two policemen saw a triangular aircraft in a farmer's field. This had white lights on each of its corners and a red light in the middle. It made for the German border, then turned around and went deeper into Belgium, where it was seen by several independent witnesses.

This craft stopped over a nearby lake, where witnesses say it shot red balls that emitted red beams. The beams would extinguish, and then the balls would cycle back up and into the UFO.

Only an hour or so later, another craft was seen, this time by thirteen policemen, as well as a number of civilians. Two policemen followed it for five miles until they lost sight of it, but it was described as also being triangular, with white lights on each corner and a red light in the middle.

All in all, seventy reported sightings that day were investigated. Nobody could find a terrestrial explanation that fit the facts.

Then, on December 1st, a witness reported a UFO hovering over the town square in Liege, which was described in an identical fashion to the others. On December 11, a young boy, along with his parents, grandparents, and sister, saw a triangular craft near their home, which hovered for fifteen minutes before leaving. Fifteen minutes after that, another craft was seen 60 miles to the west. (This was, we will no doubt have noticed, the same night as the sighting by the Amonds.)

These continued into the spring of 1990 when several more triangular objects were spotted by multiple independent witnesses. One of these was spotted over a nuclear power plant near Liege.

Perhaps strangest of all is that some of them appeared to respond to observation. One case happened in July of 1990 when a couple in their car spotted a nearby UFO with the exact same description as the others. Supposedly, the man said to his wife, "I'm going to flash my lights at it, just for fun." He did, flashing his headlights at the UFO three times.

Then, a curious thing happened: The UFO flashed its own lights three times as if acknowledging the communication. But then it tilted itself toward the car and began an approach until it was within roughly 100 yards of the vehicle.

The couple in the car were frightened almost beyond comprehension. They continued to drive, but the UFO followed them until they reached a bridge. It was only then that the craft pulled away from them and ascended the skies, leaving them be.

These are, of course, only a small sample of the bizarre events that occurred during those years. In all, it is likely that more than 2,000 sightings were reported, often by multiple independent witnesses.

Of course, as we will no doubt be familiar with by now, the vast majority of these turned out to be balloons and standard aircraft. But several hundred of the sightings remain unidentified. Some of them, like the Amond sighting, continue to boggle the mind to this day.

But given the apparent persuasiveness of some of these cases, what is it that has prevented them from going mainstream as proof of the UFO phenomenon?

"Militant Agnosticism"

In Chapter 27 of Leslie Kean's book *UFOS: UFOs - Generals, Pilots and Government Officials Go On Record*, Kean allows space for two political scientists to present their theory on what prevents instances like the Belgian wave from going mainstream.

The argument is that there are a variety of reasons for maintaining what they call the "taboo" against acknowledging UFOs as legitimate, many of which are more psychological than political (Wendt and Duvall, 2010). For example, they argue that part of the reason we refuse to think of UFOs as having an extraterrestrial origin is because the idea dethrones us from our place in the universe. The existence of a more powerful "other" basically, makes us suddenly into small fish indeed.

But there are other reasons, too, including that a more powerful "other" is a genuine physical threat. It may be psychologically beneficial to compartmentalize the possibility of a threatening, technologically advanced species, much like we compartmentalize our intrinsic terror of death.

Wendt and Duvall further suggest that perhaps there is a bit of self-preservation on the part of our governments also. They say that in order for governments to have authority, they have to give something like the appearance of being quite powerful, at least more so than their "subjects." (A more generous term might be "the governed.") The revelation that aliens exist might be enough to take some of the sheen off of the elected officials (and the unelected government lifers who surround them), which could lead to a questioning of authority that results in a dismantling of the world's power structures.

This last point is a strange one. The suggestion that governments are keeping the reality of alien life from us reads as a conspiracy theory, but more to the point, the psychological blocks to accepting the existence of alien life appear far more compelling. Perhaps we really do lack the ability to see ourselves as inferior creatures.

But even then, there remains the possibility that the Belgian wave was not a wave of UFOs at all, but something far more banal.

The Skeptic's Response

Michael Shermer is the founder of *Skeptic* magazine. He has made a name for himself over the years as a popularizer of science, and as a debunker of sorts when it comes to claims of the supernatural, paranormal, and other non-naturalistic causes.

In recent years, as interest in UFOs has increased, so has his commentary on them. In 2021, he wrote a column for his own *Skeptic* magazine that specifically addressed not only the Belgian wave, but also Kean's book.

Of particular interest to him is a rhetorical tactic used on the part of UFO enthusiasts. He makes a brief comparison between de Brouwer's testimonials regarding the Belgian wave sightings and the way Kean wrote about them in his book. Here, Shermer makes note that while de Brouwer would have said a craft was "moving very slowly," Kean would say it "appeared motionless" (Shermer, 2021, pp.17). Other examples include "without making any significant noise," shifting to "without making a sound," and "accelerating to very high speeds," becoming "speed off in the blink of an eye."

This is an important trend to make note of when doing UFO research. It suggests a kind of telephone game, where perhaps the story we are reading, after it has been filtered through a variety of different sources, may not resemble the original incident in a significant way. Or, more charitably, it may deviate from it just enough to suggest something far more astonishing than what had actually happened.

Shermer has a particular interest too in the assumptions people make about UFOs. He is keen to point out that saying a UFO is "real" is not the same thing as saying it is piloted by extraterrestrials. In fact, it is not the same as saying it is a vehicle at all—only that it exists in time and space.

His suggestion is that we employ Bayesian reasoning to determine the likelihood that a UFO has come to us from another planet (Shermer, 2021). In short, we should evaluate a situation based on "priors," meaning what we can say about the world given our current knowledge base. So, for example, if you are a homicide detective and find a man whose neck has been eaten, you should assume "animal" or "cannibal" before you assume "vampire." If someone were to tell you, then, that they saw a vampire eat the man, you should give this low credence, given that so far as you know, there has never been solid evidence proving the existence of vampires.

Shermer says this about UFOs: As he puts it, even though thousands of UFOs have been sighted at the barest minimum, not once have any of these sightings led to concrete evidence of alien life. Given this, you should give more credence to the possibility that the UFOs have a more terrestrial explanation, even as you afford a certain, smaller amount of credence to the extraterrestrial explanation.

It is not, in other words, impossible that aliens are piloting these craft. It is, however, unlikely.

Or so the story goes. Because there are some things about the Belgian wave that might force us to update those priors.

Explanations

Perhaps the most significant fact related to the Belgian wave is that it was a "wave." As Kean (2010) says, most UFO sightings are single events—one person or one group of people sees one thing. The lack of repeatability is part of what keeps the UFO phenomenon from being studied and, therefore, what keeps it marginalized.

However, the Belgian wave featured an enormous number of individual sightings seen by a large number of people. This meant, especially if the wave were to continue, that the odds of obtaining photographic or video evidence were greater than under normal circumstances. But if not, then there was, at least, a larger sample of information to work with than is usually the case.

Furthermore, even as it never became clear what exactly these UFOs were, the investigation into them did appear to at least weed out what the UFOs were *not* (Kean, 2010, chapter 1).

De Brouwer, who led the investigation, said that the going theory among researchers was that these were American stealth fighters, perhaps of an experimental variety, performing maneuvers inside Belgian airspace. But as de Brouwer notes, these exercises would have been cleared with the Belgian government unless the Americans had decided to violate a number of international laws with no discernible benefit. So, as he said, this was not an adequate explanation for what people were seeing.

This was further confirmed by USAF documents released as part of an FOIA request. The Air Force itself looked into the issue around the time of the sightings and said, in fact, that there were no American flights entering Belgian airspace without permission.

But if conventional aircraft was ruled out, then what did the investigation say was the cause of all of this?

Yet again, as with every one of these investigations, nobody could say with any certainty what exactly these things were. There was no evidence that they were from outer space and no evidence that they were conventional aircraft. There was no evidence that a mass hysteria had occurred nor that this was all the product of an enormous hoax. (Although some individual sightings were undoubtedly hoaxes.)

Eventually, the Belgian wave ended, just like all the others—the foo fighters, Roswell, everything. Still, humanity was left with more questions than answers.

But whatever the case, it was clear that the UFO phenomenon was much more global than it may have seemed previously. It was not just confined to the borders of superpowers or states at war. It had occurred within the quiet lands of Belgium, the home of the European Union.

From there, it would only spread further.

Chapter 9:

Africa's Ariel Phenomenon—The Zimbabwe School Encounter

A Close Encounter of the Third Kind.

This is more than just a sighting of a strange craft; it is not just the presence of lights in the sky or over someone's property. This is one step further into the unknown, the strange, the mysterious. It is a further alienation from what we consider reality—the kind of experience that changes one irreparably.

It is an encounter with not just the vehicles but their occupants—the creatures who some say have come to us across great distances, from other worlds. Humanoid in many ways—inhuman in others.

Surely, this is the kind of experience that would get one laughed out of polite society. Yet, some cases of a close encounter of the third kind are puzzling almost beyond conception. These cases not only tell of otherworldly beings appearing before us but in ways that defy simple explanations.

It is with one of the most compelling of these cases that we concern ourselves here.

This case not only brings us further into the depths of this strange phenomenon but into far murkier waters, so far as our assumptions are concerned. Whatever our previous understanding of UFOs—their origins, their motives—cases like this one complicate things to an impossible degree. They challenge whatever our preconceived notions were. They make us rethink the entire project.

Because why would a race that has previously concerned itself with nuclear weapons and Cold War superpowers suddenly reveal itself to a group of schoolchildren in Zimbabwe? And when they did, why did they look nothing like we have come to expect?

The Account

It happened in September 1994 at the Ariel School in Ruwa, Zimbabwe (Mack, 1999). It was morning recess, and approximately sixty children aged 9–10 appeared to see something beyond the school perimeter.

They approached it, whatever it was. As they did, some of the older kids saw them move outside of the school grounds and decided to investigate.

The older kids saw what the younger ones had found. They ran to tell their teachers.

The teachers were in a meeting at the time. Despite the children's insistence that there was *something* out there by the schoolyard, the teachers dismissed all of this as youthful imagination or even a prank.

By the time the children convinced them to at least come look, whatever it was the children had seen was gone. There was nothing there but trees and, beyond those, sand.

Over the next few days, a number of bizarre occurrences happened. For one, the children appeared to all tell the same story (Smith, 2004). This story was not only consistently told in the same way but by multiple children, suggesting that perhaps something really did happen.

But then the children drew pictures of what they had seen. What was in those pictures horrified the teachers enough to take seriously the possibility that the students had seen something incredible.

According to the story, while the kids were out at recess, they spotted a UFO, along with several other smaller ones, that landed nearby. But while this alone would have been worth investigating, this time, there was an added element: The children claimed that they had seen humanoid figures emerge from the crafts.

But these were not the gray aliens we have come to expect. These humanoids were, instead, darker-skinned with long, black hair. Most of them, too, had large eyes, and one child described a humanoid with eyes low down on the creature's face.

The humanoids did nothing strange in themselves. But after some period, probably mere minutes, the children said that the UFO and its inhabitants either "disappeared" or went up into the sky as if on a whirlwind. It was then that they ran inside to tell the teachers what they had seen.

All in all, sixty children witnessed this. Since their stories were so remarkably similar and consistent, an investigation ensued.

Investigation

The incident made its way into the lap of Dr. John E. Mack, a psychologist with an interest in UFO sightings and abductions. As it happened, he had already scheduled a trip to Africa, and so decided to pay the school a visit and interview the children about what they had seen (Mack, 1999).

He interviewed twelve of the children involved and found they all told the same story. Mack described the school as very postcolonial British, meaning that there was much discipline among the students, who replied to his questions conscientiously. He was also able to interview the headmaster and attend a class where the incident was discussed.

Mack pressed one of the students about the possibility that perhaps one of the children had played a prank, and now everyone was playing along. This student responded that she could see how it would appear that way, but that was not what had happened. In other words, she stuck with the version of events that every other child had related to him.

Despite the nature of the episode itself, there was nothing about how the children discussed it that would indicate that anything other than the version of events described is what had happened.

Perhaps lending further credence to its veracity is the emotional effect the sighting had on the children. Mack relates that many of them reported having troubling dreams and persistent fears relating to the incident (Mack, 1999). But more than that, many of the children, as they related the events of that day, appeared to recall the incident with a mixture of nervous fascination and great terror (Mack, 1999).

One of the students even described the beings as "evil." Although Mack points out that this was purely because of the "otherness" of the beings, this is telling in itself. The children appeared to understand on a very instinctual level that what they had encountered was something wholly *other*.

The eyes of these creatures held a particular fascination. Many of the students described the eyes in particular detail, especially since they seemed to be pitch black with no pupils. Along with the dark bodies of the creatures, this no doubt helped to give the impression of something sinister.

Mack says that this is not unusual among close encounters of the third kind. In fact, his writings on this aspect either help to clear up one of the discrepancies in this story or else complicate it to an unimaginable degree. Nonetheless, they were worth discussing.

The discrepancy in question here is the unusual appearance of the creatures compared to our expectations. The type of alien being that comes to mind first tends to be the typical "gray" alien, such as the EBE we discussed in the chapter on Roswell. These are the type with large eyes and heads, stout bodies, and long arms, usually with slits for a nose. Yet, the ones in Zimbabwe were dark and with long hair.

Mack says that in his experience interviewing people after alleged encounters with alien beings, there are, in fact, a wide variety of types of creatures—at least, so goes the various claims on the subject. Meaning that some people report encounters with blond, Nordic-type beings, some still with beings that resemble a praying mantis, and still others who claim to have come in contact with reptilian creatures (Mack, 1999).

None of this should be taken to mean that we are visited by a variety of alien species, perhaps from a variety of different worlds. There are, of course, theories that posit this exact scenario, most notably in the work of David Icke. However, experiences with various types of creatures do not exclude the possibility of a psychological explanation. In essence, they could be mental constructs.

In any case, while the appearance of the humanoids in the Zimbabwe encounter may be shocking to us, it is important to note that reports of the appearance of alien beings do not conform to a specific type. The fact that these humanoids were allegedly black and had long hair is not, therefore, surprising.

However, beyond the binary choice of "true encounter with an alien being" and "psychological manifestation," there is another possibility worth our consideration. That is, whether the testimonies of these children can be taken as exemplary or whether, given the sources, they should be approached with caution.

Explanations

The question of the credibility of child witnesses is not an idle one. It is one that has serious implications for several fields of study, including the law, and, in the case of the Zimbabwe encounter, has the potential to upend the entire project.

For example, there is the issue of how children understand numbers. In one real-world case (forgive the morbid example, but it is illustrative), a four-year-old girl named Jenny, whose parents had been separated, complained that her father had molested her a number of times (Saywitz, 1988). This case made it to court, where a lawyer asked Jenny how many times her father had done this to her. In response, Jenny held up both hands, fingers spread wide.

The lawyer asked her if that meant ten times. Jenny then raised two fingers. The lawyer asked if it was two times. Jenny said no, it was five. The lawyer became frustrated and said, "Well, which is it? Ten, two, or five?"

The judge had the admirable idea to ask Jenny if she knew how to count to ten. Jenny said she did and then rhymed off the numbers from 1–10 proudly. This appeared to demonstrate that Jenny did, in fact, have an understanding of numbers and could credibly relate how many times an event had occurred.

However, this is not the case. Some research indicates that children can rhyme off numbers, but in the same way that people memorize song lyrics: by rote. This does not indicate that a child has an understanding of how numbers relate to things in the world, nor how many times an event has occurred. In other words, knowing how to count does not reveal a depth of knowledge but only an ability to memorize.

How children cope with trauma is also interesting. Children who are expected to be depressed, for example, will behave as if depressed on a witness stand. How they *present* their symptoms can then change depending on what is expected of them. While their memories tend to be fairly good, they tend to be less complete than an adult's, making them unreliable. Lawyers who interview children in court often compensate for the gaps in memory by asking leading questions, even if they do so unintentionally. That children seem to respond to the needs of adults by giving them what they ask for, as in the case above, of a child appearing depressed, makes getting accurate information from them all the more perilous.

With that in mind, we should examine one possible alternative explanation for what happened.

Oliver D. Smith (2004) suggests that the event can be explained with something as simple as a "dust devil." This is a kind of tornado that occurs in the desert. They vary in size from about one meter across to over a thousand meters, and, lo and behold, they bear several similarities to the phenomenon of a UFO landing if misinterpretation on the part of the children is considered possible.

To begin with, more than one child involved described the UFO as "going round and round." This would be consistent with the motions of a dust devil, of course, but additionally, one of the children said that the UFO did not appear to touch the ground but instead hovered over it. Since a dust devil can form from the ground (unlike tornadoes, which require clouds) and can move around, they can give the appearance of hovering.

Finally, several of the children reported a "gust of wind" as the UFO left. That this could have come from a dust devil is quite obvious, considering the dust devil is itself a formation of wind, which can form a gust as it dissipates.

Of course, even if we assume a dust devil accounts for the appearance of the UFO, there are still the humanoids to consider. How can a sand tornado create what appear to be black, hairy creatures with deep black eyes?

The answer to this is surprisingly intuitive. At least two of the children reported that the aliens resembled something like "branches" from a tree. Several of their drawings, after the fact, depicted the creatures as looking conspicuously like branches.

The creatures, according to Smith's explanation, were not creatures at all but tree branches that had been caught in the whirlwind. They may have had fruit hanging off of them, which gave them a kind of alien appearance. In the heat of the moment, seen by a large gathering of children, they were misinterpreted.

We might add to this by saying that the children's memories became distorted by their feelings of terror, and perhaps also after having conversed with one another. The final piece of the puzzle might be that they recognized the answers expected of them by the researchers, which further morphed the stories into something much more sinister.

So says the more terrestrial explanation.

But is it true?

Complications

Despite all this, something remains resonant about this encounter.

As Mack says (1999), these encounters pose questions beyond the base material one. In other words, the question of whether this was a material encounter that existed in reality might, in fact, be of secondary importance. Rather, there are whole other vistas of possibility that are opened by the mere contemplation of these occurrences.

For example, Mack points out that there is a phenomenological character to encounters with the unknown that may be useful. In the case of these children seeing otherworldly beings by their school, the witnesses, despite their young age, were suddenly forced to confront the possibility that there is much more to the world than they had imagined. They were made to think of not just other worlds but other kinds of entities beyond the human. Even if it was a negative experience, it was still one of transcendence.

This is similar to what people go through when they have all manner of anomalous experiences. For example, Mack points to faith healing, apparitions, and crop circles as things that happen in the world that force us into the position of thinking well outside of ourselves—whether or not these things have a terrestrial explanation.

In this way, Mack suggests that perhaps a material explanation will always remain elusive. But there is another, more mysterious manner in which a material explanation might not be available to us, which is worth noting.

Mack points to a variety of philosophies that posit a kind of "third zone" of reality beyond thought and matter. What he means by this is that these are not subjective states or objective truths but something entirely different. Some of this is suggested by the theory of the multiverse, in which many realities coexist with one another. But it is also the realm in which the more bizarre phenomena we have occasional brushes with actually reside.

Access to this world, he says, happens through a kind of advanced stretching of consciousness, what he calls opening the "heart's mind." It is through this action that a person can gain entry into the world not just of aliens, but gods, monsters, and spirits.

Furthermore, if this realm does exist, it poses quite a problem for a reductive, materialist view of reality. No longer is it the case that we live in a world of dead matter, but in a world where genuinely strange possibilities exist. These possibilities—all the things that do not fit but happen anyway—intersect with our world on occasion, but in doing so, they reveal the multidimensional nature of reality itself.

This idea of a realm beyond the scope of our observations is not new, of course. Mack points to Eastern traditions like Hinduism for evidence of this, but there are plenty of Western ones we can throw in there as well. For example, the Celtic people believed in the Other World, which was where the faeries lived and could be accessed by, say, crossing a stream. Even the Christian tradition talks of heaven as a kind of dimension outside the material, where one can enter into a more direct communion with God.

Mack's idea, however, is much more postmodern than that. He seems to consider this place as the source of all strange happenings, such that all of our ideas about cryptozoology, religion, and magic are all true. Much like the Hollow Earth for some people, it is a place where Bigfoot can exist comfortably alongside the Mothman while also being the source of psychic phenomena, alien beings, and miracles.

***

Whether or not we take this idea as literally true, it does perhaps require us to think outside the box for a moment.

Is it possible that when we talk about aliens, we are not talking about material entities that come from other planets but something much more mysterious?

Consider that up until the Belgian wave, UFOs tended to be seen during epochal wars, hovering around advanced technology like nuclear weapons and appearing largely within the borders of the two superpowers. The assumption then was that these beings were concerned with what was most important: the technology that was the most advanced, the countries with the most power, and the events whose conclusion would determine the future of human history.

But why did they appear in Belgium? Why in the Belgian woods or over people's property?

And why did they appear near a school in a small town in southern Africa?

Perhaps our understanding of their motives needs to be revised. Perhaps it was only a coincidence that we found them where we had found them previously. Perhaps they are not concerned with our centers of power and technology at all but with something very different.

In fact, maybe their intentions are purely hostile. But if that were the case, then surely they would have attacked us by now.

But then again, maybe they already have.

Chapter 10:

Russia's Cosmos of Mysteries—From Tunguska to Contemporary Sightings

It began as a sleepy day in the Siberian summer.

It was 1908. Quiet, no doubt, and warm, considering the Siberian summer climate. Maybe there were birds chirping and deer running between the trees. Local villages, the ones that surrounded the woods, were likely going about their business as if everything was perfectly normal.

Because it was perfectly normal. At least for a while.

Sometime that morning, a crazy thing happened. An enormous light, as bright as the sun, lit up the sky (Bauer, 2016). Local villagers saw the source of this light: a streak careening through the sky, hurtling toward the Siberian forest.

It struck with incredible speed. A deafening sound roared from the impact, sounding like artillery. A ball of flame took up the entire sky, and a shockwave ripped through the air, shattering windows hundreds of miles away.

By the time the dust was cleared, the air would have been filled with smoke and gas. The woods would have looked as though somebody had burned it to the ground. Shattered trees were scattered everywhere, and the Earth was littered with the carcasses of destroyed animals.

The blast killed three people. And no wonder—it was perhaps a thousand times more powerful than the bomb dropped on Hiroshima. It was, and remains, the most devastating impact on the Earth's surface in recorded history. To find one more damaging, you would have to look all the way back through prehistory.

So what was it? An asteroid impact? A comet? That it came from space is not in question, since there were few man-made vehicles in the air at the time. The devastation it caused too seems to suggest something enormous, falling to our planet at an incredible speed.

Yet, what if there is another explanation? Could it be that the Tunguska event, as it is now called, was the result of no asteroid at all but something much more extraordinary?

Could it even have been something from beyond the bounds of imagination?

A Crashed Spaceship

Picture a spaceship of enormous size. Maybe the mothership from *Childhood's End* or *Independence Day*. Maybe it was hurtling through our solar system on its way somewhere else. Maybe it was orbiting our humble planet, observing from a distance. Perhaps only a few years prior, they had been sending airships down to get a closer look.

What would happen if a ship underwent a catastrophic malfunction while in Earth's orbit? If it tilted too far in the direction of the planet, it would find itself sucked toward it via gravity. It would possibly catch fire in the atmosphere even before it reached terminal velocity.

If it had enough mass, its impact explosion might be several orders of magnitude greater than that of an atomic bomb.

The idea that the explosion was caused by a fallen alien spaceship was not invented for the purpose of this chapter. It is, however, a fairly prominent—although admittedly fringe—theory amongst people interested in this strange occurrence.

One of the more famous books on the subject is called *The Fire Came By* (Oberg, 1978). Although written by two drama critics, the thesis of the book is quite simple: The only plausible explanation for the Tunguska event was that it was caused by a falling, nuclear-powered, interstellar spaceship. To them, this was a ship trying to land on our planet until something went wrong. That "something" led to an event that eerily resembled an atomic explosion.

The authors of *The Fire Came By* made the media rounds after publication. They insisted that they had, if not the final word on the subject, then at least that they had advanced the cause of scientific inquiry.

Although, to do this, they relied on some perhaps dubious evidence regarding the state of things at the impact site.

In fact, while several enthusiasts claim that the event is absolute proof that UFOs not only exist but are of immense size and with incredible capabilities, some of the evidence discussed in relation to the event is, to put it bluntly, made up. For example, a persistent myth says that large amounts of radiation were discovered at the site many years after the fact. However, this is, alas, just not so. In fact, the only radiation discovered at the site can be accounted for as fallout from nearby Soviet H-bomb tests.

Additionally, when the writers of *The Fire Came By* were pressed for evidence of their claims, they were remarkably cagey. According to Oberg, who debated them on the radio, they seemed unaware of any of the evidence *against* their claims at all. They seemed to have done little to no research, beyond some wild speculations about the possibility of a nuclear mothership crashing into eastern Russia.

None of which prevents the persistence of the idea that *The Fire Came By* is correct. As Oberg points out, this theory seems to have a remarkable ability to resurface again and again, no matter how many times it is put down. In this way, it is a sort of Terminator of Tunguska event theories.

But if that is true, then what are we to call the next candidate? Is it the Cthulhu of Tunguska event theories? The Azathoth?

How else to describe the proper level of cosmic dread we should feel if it were to be true?

Black Hole

The black hole is the sublime figure of cosmic terror. Unthinkably massive, infinitely black, bending space and time with the sheer force of its gravity—what else in the universe is as mind-numbing as these astronomical reality eaters?

Yet, these are perhaps not the only types of black holes in existence. One theory is that there are tiny black holes scattered throughout the cosmos. Many of these could have been formed right at the Big Bang (Time, 1973) and been sent hurtling through space. Still others could be fragments formed after two black holes collided with one another.

In the 1970s, scientists Albert Jackson and Michael Ryan relied on these tiny black holes to propose a strange solution to the problem of what hit Tunguska in 1908. According to them, it was possible that one of these tiny black holes had come close enough to Earth, that it resulted in an enormous explosion.

One of these tiny black holes, to begin with, would have the mass of about a medium-sized asteroid. Since black holes are by nature densely packed into the smallest possible space (making their frequently enormous size all the more alarming), a tiny black hole would be incredibly heavy despite being about the size of a proton.

The theory says that one of these objects came too close to Earth, which set off a kind of chain reaction. Jackson and Ryan proposed a model that uses eyewitness reports of the explosion to judge the angle at which the object (or chain reaction) entered the atmosphere and then says that, in their model, this would be the exact angle expected of such a chain reaction. This would have also led to atmospheric effects over Nova Scotia, which they said should be investigated: Did anyone in Nova Scotia at that time see anything that resembles the kind of thing they suggest occurred at that time?

This theory has, however, also been dismissed by scientists. The reasons for this are beyond the scope of this book, but it has been suggested that Jackson and Ryan's proposal failed due to "several lines of evidence" pointing to the theory's lack of utility (Beasley and Tinsley, 1974).

But if this fact does much to ease our sense of existential terror, the next theory suggests the horror of a steampunk variety that is almost too wild to discount.

Death Ray

Nikola Tesla is a figure who borders on the legendary. Many urban legends have featured him as a kind of omnipotent figure, whose inventions are behind all manner of bizarre phenomena. He was even featured in the film *The Prestige*, which, while not featuring him as a central character, did feature him as a kind of *primary* character, whose inventions turned out to be *the* significant mover in the plot.

It is not surprising then to find him possibly lurking behind the Tunguska event. In many ways, it was only a matter of time. But the manner in which he may have been the cause of this mysterious event is nonetheless one which beggars belief.

Especially since the theory involves the creation of a death ray.

Around the time of the Tunguska event, Tesla became convinced that electricity could be transmissible through the air (Theunredacted, 2016). His experiments with this theory were funded by none other than J.P. Morgan, and led to the development of several devices, which Tesla was sure would prove his theory correct.

After numerous failures, however, Morgan was forced to pull Tesla's funding, leaving the inventor in utter ruin. This state of affairs led to Tesla's nervous breakdown, after which he became quite desperate.

According to the theory, Tesla devised a way to make his machine known to the public. He had already hypothesized that if electricity could be transmitted through the air, then any machine that pulled this off could be used as a weapon. Furthermore, he thought a weapon of significant power could destroy a target hundreds of miles away.

Then, around the time of the Tunguska event, he began sending cryptic messages to Arctic explorers, telling them to "watch for signals." He wrote to himself that his imaginings were not dreams but that he had devised a way to make whole environments uninhabitable through the use of this awful weapon.

Tesla began to dream even bigger. He said he could light up the entire ocean so that the *Titanic* accident would never happen again, and he could light up the entire sky if he wished.

Then came the Tunguska event.

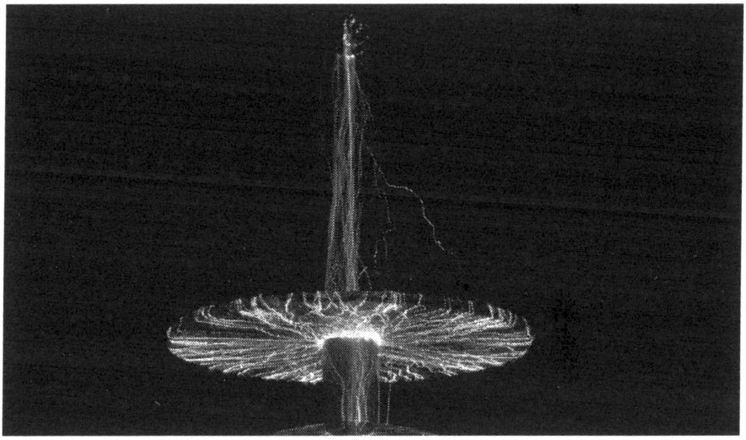

But could Tesla have done this? The prevailing theory among scientists is that the event was due to an asteroid or a comet. This, they say, explains everything from the sky brightening before the explosion to the explosion itself. For the proponents of metaphysical materialism, this is as sufficient as it is obvious.

Yet, there are ways in which this does not make sense. If an asteroid did hit Tunguska, *why was there no impact crater?*

This is a fact that bears repeating: *There is no impact crater at the site of the explosion.*

Nothing hit the ground that day. An explosion did happen, of course—there is ample evidence to support this. But nothing hit the ground. Nothing *collided.*

If Tesla had developed a death ray, there is little doubt that it would not have left an impact crater since it would not require one thing to collide with another. A death ray, by definition, would use an enormous transfer of electricity to a given area in order to destroy a specific target or targets. Might this explain why there was an enormous explosion? Did he perhaps target the trees in the forest with the intention of using this as a publicity stunt?

Then again, there is the problem of power. A stunt like that would require more electricity than the whole of the New York City power grid could supply (Theunredacted, 2016). Tesla relied on this grid to power his inventions. He did not have enough energy at his disposal to explode the Siberian woods.

This fact alone is enough to kill speculation that a death ray was involved. But by now the question might be asked: Why is it so hard to figure out what was responsible for this? We have gone over four possible scenarios, including that an asteroid hit the area. None of them have so far proven adequate.

But why?

An Impossible Task

The explosion occurred in 1908. The first expedition to investigate it happened in 1927 (Tedesco, 2024).

It was nearly two decades before anyone decided to look into what happened. At that time, the Soviets sent a research scientist named Leonid Alekseyevich Kulik, although there was very little material for him to work with.

His findings, which were gathered over several expeditions over a period of three years, found that even two decades after the fact, very little was growing in the place of the destroyed plant life. Trees remained shattered, scattered all throughout the woods. It was these trees which led him to the epicenter, the pinpoint away from which all the trees faced.

What about the epicenter? We have said already that there was no crater. Kulik was the first to discover this, as he came across a marshy bog but nothing else.

Still, the amount of information he could have gathered so long after the fact was limited—at least, more limited than if someone had looked into it much sooner. Any explanation regarding the cause of this event would be hidden behind temporal layers, too numerous to peel back.

Then, there is the nature of the state we are talking about. The Iron Curtain was called such because of the high level of secrecy within the Soviet Union. Very little information got out, and for the citizens within those borders, very little got in either.

This was an isolated empire, and everyone within was themselves isolated. Its own UFO program had little interest in communicating with the public. Its citizens were routinely lied to and manipulated by the government. Virtually everyone was spying on everyone else, leaving little room for much besides paranoia.

Anyone curious about the event between the years 1922 and 1989 would find themselves up against the Iron Curtain. No information would be forthcoming, even if the Soviets did possess it.

Who is to say that beyond those dark layers of deception and paranoia, the Soviets did *not* have that information? Could they have hidden it somewhere and lost it as the USSR fell, if not before? Given the amount of secrecy within the Soviet Union, how will we ever know?

It is in times like this that the mind flails outward to find an explanation. The black hole in the center of the question is intolerable. Nobody can withstand not knowing, least of all, when it is something as momentous as this.

Is this the time to fill in the blanks with speculation?

Science and Reason

What if the explosion was due to something extraterrestrial?

The fact that a nuclear-powered mothership did not crash in Siberia may tell us something. But it may tell us nothing. It may tell us that two men grew intoxicated by sci-fi speculations and wrote a book to express their sense of awe and wonder at the limitless potential of the cosmos. More cynically, it could be that they knew how to make a buck and concocted the strangest yarn they could think of, appealing to the public's taste in the unusual.

It could be that they *wanted* it to be true as well. Just as it could be true that people *wanted* to believe that Tesla made a death ray and accidentally unloaded it near a poor Siberian village.

But what of the critics, the skeptics? Can we not say that they, too, *want* their worldview to be true? To write for publications like the *Skeptical Inquirer* is to commit oneself to a set of propositions about the world we live in: that it is material, predictable, studyable, and so on. Faced with the possibility that the world is something other than these things, and one would no doubt collapse under the strain of embarrassment.

From within the tension between science and speculation, where are we to stake our ground? In other words, How do we *know* anything?

Of the Tunguska event, we know very little. We know that something happened and that whatever it was, it led to an explosion that destroyed whole swathes of woodland and killed three people. But beyond this, we face the unknown, the mysterious. We reach an event horizon, after which all we have is speculation.

Perhaps the unknown is merely another horizon for us to run toward. New tools, new technology, and new methods of research may bring us closer to it, and with that bring more of the unknown into the light of the known.

But perhaps the unknown is something different. Perhaps the unknown is not something we have yet to know but something unknowable. An encounter with the limits of our knowledge can be a stark reminder of just how limited we are—and will always be. From that vantage point, the only thing we can do is speculate.

The Tunguska event is what happens when the unknown makes contact with the material. An event that is itself unknowable enters the world's space and brings chaos. From there, it retreats off into the wilderness, never to reveal itself again.

Tunguska is one in a series of unknowns. Ancient aliens. Foo fighters. Roswell. Intrusions into the world of facts and values, strange breaks in the causal matrix.

And so: What if the explosion was due to something extraterrestrial?

How much longer can we stand not to know?

Chapter 11:

Latin American Legends—

Chilbolton and Beyond

Varginha, 1996.

We are in Brazil. This is the only majority Portuguese-speaking country in the Americas, a country renowned for its sensuality, strong family ties, and tempestuous politics. It is often quite hot and, in January, rainy.

It was also the place where a number of people saw a devil. A horned, red-eyed creature, possibly scared, certainly threatening. A devil, if the rumors are true, that was covered up by the Brazilian government.

But was it? And if not, what happened?

Coyame, Mexico. 1974.

The desert. Almost unbearably hot. A strange ship collided with a commercial aircraft and crashed into the sand.

Locals tell the story of how it was covered up by the Americans—how the Yankees blew up the evidence, including Mexican soldiers.

But did they? And if not, what happened?

Mexico City, 2014.

Mexican military officials hunt for drug-smuggling aircraft in the dead of night. But what they find instead are several UFOs darting through the sky at unbelievable speeds.

But did they? And if not, what happened?

These and more are the stories of Latin American UFO sightings, visitations by creatures from elsewhere, in cities big and small, surrounded by heat, desert, rainforest, and the region's characteristic mix of Indigenous folklore and Catholicism.

But then, something curious: As far away as Great Britain, a series of detailed, eerie crop circles are found that capture the attention of the island's inhabitants. Crop circles that are not just complex but perhaps contain hints of something much bigger and much stranger.

But why bring these into the conversation at all? Surely, a UFO-type event as far away as Great Britain can't have any connections to Brazilian devils.

Yet, what if they are connected? What if we can learn about the nature of the Latin American sightings by comparing them with these odd events in Great Britain?

More to the point: What if, through doing so, we can identify the nature of the phenomenon itself?

Brazil

It was January 1996 in Varginha. Three witnesses—between the ages of 14 and 22—came upon a terrible sight: a hairless, horned creature with oily brown skin and red eyes—a creature they referred to later as a "devil" (Harvey, 2024).

This set off a chain reaction. Several other residents came forward to say that they, too, had seen this devil skulking around the neighborhood. Almost everyone who reported seeing this creature stated that they knew it to be not from this world but from *somewhere else.*

From there, the reports continued, only to increase the intensity of their claims. Residents told of UFOs streaking across the sky, of course, but to this standard detail were added several that boggled the mind. These claims included the possibility that the Brazilian military was rounding up extraterrestrials and bringing them to the local hospital for surveillance.

If true, these would be the most incredible stories on record. It would mean that the Brazilian government had living aliens in their possession and that one of them had apparently gotten loose and was roaming through people's yards.

Of course, it was only a matter of time before the government was pressed for answers. What did they know about the red-eyed devil? Were they hiding aliens in the hospital—and if not, what did residents see being carried into the hospital on a stretcher?

According to the government, the explanations for both of these events were, in fact, quite pedestrian: The red-eyed devil was a local homeless man named Mudinho, and the residents had seen something carried into the hospital on a stretcher—except that it was a couple with dwarfism on their way to give birth.

Yet, there are those who claim this is all misdirection. At least one of the initial witnesses swears that what she saw was no man. She says she ran home, convinced she saw the devil, and drew a picture for her mom. This picture depicted a humanoid, yes—but one with three horns spread over his forehead.

Other reports from around the same time complicate matters somewhat. A man claims he saw a cigar-shaped craft in the sky only a week before the first sighting of the town's devil. Not only that, but he claims the craft had smoke billowing from it as if it was damaged. It also seemed to be losing altitude as if crashing.

As he told the story, he walked to where he was sure the craft had crashed. He found it smashed in an open field, with debris scattered everywhere. A foul smell overpowered him also, only getting stronger as he approached the bulk of the UFO.

Before he could get too close, however, military personnel emerged and swarmed him. They instructed him to leave immediately, then forced him to comply.

His story is not the only one, either. Several others saw a crashing ship around the same time. Then, within a week, townspeople were claiming they saw an inhuman creature.

Is there a connection? Did a ship crash nearby, and the creature everyone saw was no homeless man at all but a stranded and scared alien—perhaps navigating his way through this hostile environment, trying to get himself to safety?

Let's stay for a second on how the witnesses described the creature. As of 2013, Brazil has the largest percentage of Catholics anywhere in the world (Liu, 2013). Catholicism, as we discussed in our chapter on the Middle Ages, has a well-established hierarchy of spiritual beings, including angels and demons. Medieval Catholicism especially had strong beliefs related to how "demons" or "devils" prowled about the Earth, seeking the ruin of souls.

That a majority Catholic country would interpret a menacing, non-human creature as a devil should be no surprise. We have already described the similarities between demon possession and abduction by aliens. Perhaps the witnesses to this event in Brazil made a similar mental comparison and declared the being they had seen as a devil.

But then again, maybe the reverse is true. Maybe what we understand as aliens are actually demons. Maybe what skeptics understand as hallucinations, telephone games, and misinterpretations is actually something far more sinister.

Coyame, Mexico

Mexico's Roswell occurred in 1974 when *something* crashed in the desert. This area was, for mysterious reasons perhaps, known for its numerous plane crashes (Javier and Natera, 2012). So, it may have been no surprise when a plane flying over the area collided with something mid-air.

The surprise came later. The craft—whatever it was—crashed in the desert, where it was found by some of the locals. It appeared, in at least one telling, to resemble a flying saucer but was otherwise in a terrible state.

Soon enough, an American Special Forces team arrived on the scene. They forced everyone to leave, then torched all the evidence of the crash. This included torching several Mexican soldiers, who did not survive.

The official story, meanwhile, runs like this:

Drug runners, flying over the desert, collided with a mountain and crashed. The plane—or two, depending on the version—landed in a nearby ranch, which led to one of the passengers burning alive.

No American soldiers. No aliens. No UFO.

But if that version is true, then what would lead witnesses to interpret it as the former series of events? Could it be that animosity between the Mexicans and Americans, along with some knowledge of clandestine operations performed against Cartel members, mixed up with UFO folklore to become the unofficial story?

Mexico City

Here, we find ourselves in the largest city in North America. Home of the luchadores, the favorite destination of Jack Kerouac—a cultural titan and an ancient city.

Also, as it happens, a city with a high crime rate. In 2022, for example, there were 3.5 million crimes committed (Statistica, 2023). Additionally, for every 100 thousand inhabitants, 46 thousand incidents of crime were committed. This, plus the stories about cartels and their government's efforts to contain the spread of violence, makes Mexico City something of a dangerous place.

Then, in 2014, Mexican Air Force pilots spotted 11 UFOs while searching for drug smuggling planes (Smith, 2004). They said that the encounter scared them, as they had never seen anything like that before. They insisted that the footage they recorded could not be altered and that it was genuine. In doing so, they received support from Mexican UFOlogists, who insisted that the military would not make fraudulent claims about UFOs.

Of course, there are other explanations beyond fraud. Some skeptics insisted that what the pilots saw—points of light in infrared—could have been from a meteor breaking up. Others said the light could have come from flares shot off at a local oil field. Ball lightning, too, has been offered as an explanation.

In fact, according to *Skeptic* magazine (Smith, 2004), it seems as though flares really are the culprit here. When the lights in the footage are compared to a 3D model of flares being set off in the same location, the model is almost identical to the footage. There was, obviously, an oil field nearby, and geolocated satellite footage appears to confirm that this oil field was, in fact, setting off flares at that time.

But then—*so what?* What if the terrestrial explanation really is the correct one?

The men who saw the lights are engaged in a fight against the cartels. The cartels are notorious for using an inhuman level of violence, such that it can be easy to see them as something Other Than Human. The military is unlikely to penetrate the cartels as well, making them a bona fide Other in many, many ways.

What is the cartel, in that sense, if not a kind of alien being? Is it not understandable, perhaps, that a disturbance in the normal sequence of events is interpreted as coming from an unhuman source when the enemy they are looking for appears to be just that? Is this not just another case of someone projecting their fears and desires onto something they do not understand—a kind of Rorschach test where the ink blob constantly looks something like a threatening, alien entity?

The lights, in other words, were an unknown—and the high-strung minds of active duty soldiers filled in the blanks with a metaphor of their worst fear.

Crop Circles

Over five thousand years ago, the first steps were made toward building an unusual monument. It was built by a people hardly known to history except through rumors and whispers. These mysterious people erected large slabs of stone amidst a cold, foggy landscape. They did this for reasons unknown and unknowable, themselves people lost to the darkness of time.

Were these the same people who sacrificed people in the Wicker Man? Did they build enormous effigies filled with animals and a human people in its skull, only to set it on fire as a gift to the gods? Which gods did they worship, and how many?

They are not people we will ever meet, whether in person or through writing, as they never wrote anything down.

All we know is they were the early inhabitants of the land of Great Britain. Although their ways have come and gone, there are still little remnants of them poking through the British cultural psyche.

For example, in the late 1970s, a series of events in the English countryside suddenly put the town of Chilbolton and others on the map. A number of what are called "crop circles" made appearances in a number of fields, particularly wheat. In essence, these are shapes, drawings, or something similar that have been made in the fields, usually over a short time span and featuring an abnormal level of detail.

In fact, the details in these crop circles are more than a little staggering.

Several of these drawings in the fields depicted things like the mathematical Julia set (Stables, 2021), a fractal that represents the boundary of the set of points in the complex plane that do not escape to infinity under iterative applications of a particular complex function. Sound complicated? Imagine finding it beside Stonehenge, where it was discovered.

Another was found by an Iron Age castle and decoded by an astrophysicist, who determined it was a geometric representation of the first ten digits of pi. Another fractal was discovered that was over 900 feet long.

Some of the people who study them have said that their first encounters with the crop circles were of a spiritual nature. They had the realization that such enormously complicated figures could not have been made by people overnight. The amount of work to construct them led to a transcendental experience, where it became obvious that there were forces in the world much greater than us.

Others invoke what are called "ley lines," a concept from New Age spirituality that nonetheless has ties to Great Britain's spiritual history. These "lines" are supposed to run through spiritual sites of great importance, such as Stonehenge and Avebury. This latter site is one of the oldest religious sites in England, now a series of three stone circles. The crop circles, as it happens, are said to run through these as well, or else confirm the existence of them.

In other words, there is a direct, immediate connection between the crop circles and the artifacts of the English pagan tradition.

That crop circles are supposed to be connected too with UFO activity is well-known. If true, then the theory might suggest that aliens have something in common with English religious sites like Stonehenge. Perhaps, since the building of Stonehenge remains mysterious to us, it could be that the authors of the famous site are not from this Earth at all.

While some discount E.T. involvement, believers insist that perhaps the humans who make the crop circles have tapped into something much more otherworldly. It could be that they have entered a strange type of conscious state, one that allows them to discover complex mathematical images that were previously unknown to them and then imprint them in the wheat fields.

From there, we might extrapolate: Could it be that beings from other worlds are commandeering the minds of these British farmers? Perhaps this is much like the Oracle at Delphi, possessed by Apollo and gifted with foresight.

If the ancient astronaut theory is true, and the aliens really are our ancient gods…

The connections between the ancient pagan sources of Great Britain and the English understanding of visitations might now be obvious. But there is yet another angle.

At least two of the men who began making crop circles in the 1970s are known to us: their names are Doug and Dave (Wilson, 2022). They have described in detail how they made these figures in the night, all, they said, for a laugh. If they are telling the truth, then crop circles are nothing more than an elaborate prank pulled on the credulous UFO "experts" and the profit-driven media.

So what are we to make of the fact that this explanation is dismissed by believers?

This is from *The New York Times* (Wilson, 2022):

> Mr. Andrews, 76, claims to have invented the term "crop circles" after first viewing one in July 1983 and admits he has since made a good living from the phenomenon, having sold hundreds of thousands of books and traveled the world, giving up to three paid lectures or public appearances a week.
>
> He said his invitations to speak "tailed off straight away" after the confessions by Mr. Bower and Mr. Chorley, but he continues to monitor crop circles and insists he is "more convinced than ever" that there are nonhuman causes.
>
> "Where is the proof that all of them are man-made?" said Mr. Andrews, quickly adding that even if they are all man-made, he believes the people making the circles have unwittingly "been prompted by an independent nonhuman mind."

Mr. Andrews believes that England is host to something extraordinary. At the very least, an "independent, nonhuman mind" is responsible for manipulating hapless British farmers into doing their bidding. But in the most maximal sense, his feeling is that these were not made by men at all.

Rewind a moment: There was a time in history, not that long ago, when Great Britain was the largest, most powerful empire in the whole history of the world. The sun never set on the

British Empire because it was quite literally in every time zone. Its influence was, and remains, incalculable.

Even after the empire was dismantled, England continued to be a powerhouse. It gave the world the Beatles, the Rolling Stones, *Harry Potter*, and Guy Richie. Its cultural reach was extraordinary, even for a country that had reduced itself from spreading over the globe to a retreated perch back on its home island.

It is no secret that England is no longer even *that*. Its cultural influence is largely negligible, and its political situation has been chaotic, to say the least. Because of all this, it is no longer a dominant force on the world stage.

Maybe the desire to believe that England is a unique, one might say "magical" place, is so strong that the mind recoils at attempts to bring crop circles down to Earth. *No*, it might say, *that can't be true. This is England. This is King Arthur territory. Of course, minds greater than ours would take a special interest in the English countryside. Of course, they would want to deliver us a message. And, of course, that message is encrypted—these minds know we are just the kind of people brilliant enough to crack the code.*

At least to them up there, the sun still never sets on Jolly Ol' England.

***

Yet, again, we find ourselves at the great impasse.

It might be true that a homeless man was mistaken for a devil; that a downed drug-running plane was mistaken for a UFO; that a series of flares were interpreted by high-strung soldiers as evidence of an alien visitation; and that designs made in a wheat field by a bunch of teenagers is either a sign of England's continued lineage with its pagan history, or else a sign of its greatness and importance on the galactic stage.

But then again, it might be true that the need to be skeptical, to have one's priors confirmed, has made us project our skepticism onto something extraordinary.

The answer to that is not available. Perhaps it is perpetually unavailable. Whatever the case, it is obvious that our cultural milieu has a habit of imposing itself on the UFO phenomenon. It is almost like a creature of infinite morphological potential, able to be at once drawn from Catholicism and pre-Druidic paganism. It can be science fiction, and it can be superstition.

So, as we move further out into the world, we might ask ourselves: Just what *else* can it be?

Chapter 12:

Asia's Ancient and Modern Anomalies

Between 139 BC and 1918 AD, as many as 741 recorded UFO incidents occurred in China (Huneeus, 2010). "Recorded," that is, in the sense that someone bothered to write down that they had encountered something odd, some apparent violation of natural law that took place in the heavens.

Some of these records are in the form of strange, pithy journal entries, such as one from 32 BC that simply says, "Two moons appeared in the night sky all of a sudden." Others, however, were much more complex.

For example, this one from 905 AD (Huneeus, 2010):

> "In the middle of the night, a very large star that looked like a *dou* (a 10-liter box-like grain measuring container) suddenly appeared in the top of the sky and was floating toward the northwest. When it had reached about 30 meters above the ground, it suddenly stopped and remained still. The top of the star appeared to be burning, and red and yellow blazing flames were as high as 5 meters tall. Later the star started to serpentine. Wherever had it passed, little stars on its sides were moving toward the southeast, and they came down like raindrops that soon disappeared. Meanwhile, pale mist

> rose from the earth like bamboo thickets toward the center of the sky."

Remember that this was from the year 905. In the West, Rome had only been in its imperial period for less than a thousand years. Great Britain was not a country. Colonization of the Americas was still several centuries away. In fact, historically speaking, we are still dealing with the period we refer to as "the ancient world."

Meaning, we have entered again the realm of ancient aliens. Only now, we have moved to the other side of the world, during a time when East and West did not communicate with one another. They were isolated and independent.

Yet, each went through these same experiences: bizarre, unnatural things in the sky, seen by men and women who had no idea what to make of these things—except of course, to try and understand them through the ancient world's predilection for the otherworldly, the supernatural, and the close proximity of its gods and spirits.

But how could this happen? How could all these continents, from the Americas to Europe, to Africa, and now Asia, all have the same experiences at times when this information could not have been passed from one to the other? How could ancient people all see things in the sky that did not make sense?

How could this have continued all through China's medieval period and into the present day in Asia—all with remarkable similarities to what has been happening all over the world?

How much of this do we need to see before admitting something is going on here?

Liu Yin

Fast forward a few centuries from 905 AD.

Liu Yin has been described by some as a "hermit scholar" (Huneeus, 2010). He was a philosopher well-versed in Confucianism who believed in training the mind and investigating reality to probe it for the truth. It was this emphasis on investigating strange occurrences to discover the truth that influenced his approach to a bizarre UFO sighting in the year 1277.

The details of his sighting are almost horrifyingly modern. He says that he rose one morning—apparently while it was still dark—and looked up to the Milky Way. As he did, he saw several objects, which had five lights underneath them and strange domes over the top. They flew rapidly through the air and made zigzag patterns; some disappeared, and one more stayed even as the sun rose.

Once the sun had risen enough to provide light, Liu Yin saw that the flying object was surrounded by an immense fire. This shape was ovular and flat and descending quickly.

Liu Yin ran to get the other villagers to tell them what had happened. But by the time he roused them and brought them to the place from which he had seen the flying object, it and all the others like it were gone.

Given to philosophy, Liu Yin spent the remainder of the day trying to work out what he could have seen. But even with all his training, he could not even hazard a guess. The whole sequence of events gave him the feeling of waking from a dream, as though it was so unbelievable he almost could not believe it had happened.

He wrote down the events in the hopes that someone, in the years hence, could get to the bottom of this. Perhaps someone with greater knowledge than he would know what he had seen in the sky.

Of course, there are those who believe they do know what he had seen. The lights underneath, the dome structure over the top—how can we not think of Colonel André Amond and his wife?

It only took 700 years. But perhaps, given everything that has happened in the past century or so, we have finally solved the mystery of what happened to poor, solitary Liu Yin.

Utsuro Bune

Fast forward once again, move slightly westward, and we arrive in Japan in the 19th century. Only this time, we encounter a story straight out of *The Twilight Zone.*

In 1803, a strange, hollow ship washed on the shores of the Hitachi beach (Tanaka, 2020). From out of this ship emerged a beautiful woman who could not speak or understand Japanese and was carrying a box. Her clothes were noted as being unusual, and the ship was marked with a script none of the locals understood.

This story is cataloged in many records from the periods and has been studied extensively by Tanaka Kazuo, professor emeritus at Gifu University. In fact, before Professor Tanaka took to studying this tale, he was a professor of optics. But something about it made him pivot away from his previous specialization—and it is with that that we must concern ourselves.

In the mid-90s, a fanatical cult killed a number of people at a Tokyo subway station using deadly gas. The cult was led by a man who claimed to have the gift of prophecy and who, it was said, could fly.

Perhaps most interestingly, the senior members of this cult were not deluded and uneducated but members of Japan's scientific elite. This intrigued Tanaka, who decided to study the paranormal from a scientific perspective and began giving lectures on the subject.

It was while doing research that he came upon American UFO reports, as well as folkloric material from inside Japan. What he realized was that several hundred years before UFOs became a topic of interest in the United States, Japanese folklore had this story about what may have been a flying saucer.

The big difference, however, was that the American UFO reports were often from single eyewitnesses, with little evidence to trace. The hollow ship from Japanese folklore, however, was different: There were a lot of evidential threads one could examine, which gave it the allure of possibly having scientific value.

Japanese history attests to several encounters with hollow ships. But for Tanaka, the story of the woman in Hitachi was of greater interest because it was referenced in so many sources. For example, a book of "fantastic rumors" from 1825 mentions the encounter, and more books have collected tales from Japanese seamen during this period, especially of strange ships washing ashore.

Tanaka's initial theory was that perhaps there was a grain of truth to this story, but it had been embellished over time. For example, maybe a Russian fisherman had accidentally landed in Japan after being carried out to sea. This story may have then gotten stuck in a telephone game, only to come out the other end in the form we have been discussing. However, he not only found no evidence to corroborate this; instead, he found piles of more evidence, including an account from 1803, the year the evidence was said to occur.

Adding to this are the several drawings made of the craft from the beginning of the 19th century. These all depict an object that looks strikingly like a modern UFO, something of which Tanaka took note.

As he tells it, there are certainly many tales involving hollow ships washing ashore from Japanese folklore that one can write off as being merely stories. But this one is different. Not only did it happen relatively recently, but it happened during a time when Japan was relatively closed off. For Tanaka, this suggests that a foreign ship washing up on the beach would have been an enormous national story. That it did not become that suggests that something else must have happened.

In fact, whatever may have happened may have been *interpreted* as being like a hollow ship story. He says that this would have taken place over a short period of time. We might surmise then that if it was sufficiently outside the realm of experience for the people who encountered it, perhaps they, like everyone else we have looked at, would have understood it best in the context of an old legend. This was the version that got passed around, leading to its classification as a hollow ship story.

But if this were true, it would mean that the event itself was perhaps far more divorced from everyday reality than even this odd tale of a beautiful woman speaking an unknown language and carrying a mysterious box.

Perhaps it was something so outside the bounds of ordinary experience that describing it as it was would have been all but impossible.

Tehran

We move now into 1976 and to the mountainous regions of Iran's capital. It was here, on September 19th, that an enormous object was spotted floating above the city (Unidentified Phenomena, 2023). It was described as being possibly 100 feet in diameter, emitting a bright light and hovering in the sky.

Tehran is no small town. It is a large and major city that plays a significant role in regional politics. The UFO in question was in full view of the public. So, of course, the Iranian air force was sent to intercept whatever had entered their skies.

The Air Force dispatched two fighter jets to intercept this mysterious guest. But as the jets drew closer, they began to malfunction. Communication failure followed as if something was protecting the UFO.

The pilots drew close enough, however, to get a good look at this thing. It was described as metallic with a bright, pulsating light in its middle. Once they drew too close, however, the malfunctions became dangerous, and they were forced to pull away. Perhaps unsurprisingly, once they were a certain distance away from the UFO, their systems began working again.

Some reports on the incident suggest that several smaller UFOs detached themselves from the primary object, made some maneuvers, and then returned to their source object. These reports are controversial, however.

What is not controversial is that it was picked up on the radar. In fact, radar confirmed not only that the object was over Tehran but that it flew away at an extraordinary speed and maneuvered in ways that were puzzling to the Air Force personnel who investigated this later.

The American Defense Intelligence Agency even took an interest in it. They even produced a document detailing the events, which appears to add credibility to the fact that this was not merely a hoax or a case of mistaking a group of birds for an alien spacecraft.

But what was it then? Many people believe that this is as rock solid as evidence gets for UFOs, particularly those of extraterrestrial origin. After all, it was seen not only by civilians but by fighter pilots—and, furthermore, by the Shah's personal assistant, who was the first to notice the craft.

The Iranian government initiated an investigation into the matter, but as no official confirmation has ever come from them that they had, indeed, found an alien spaceship, it is safe to assume that the results turned out in exactly the same way as all the others we have looked into.

More papers. More documents. More time spent trying to learn the nature and origin of these things. Yet, nothing to go on, so far as the extraterrestrial hypothesis is concerned.

Even as close as they apparently got, the phenomenon remained—and remains—elusive.

Modern China and Spycraft

If the first Cold War saw an increase in the number of UFO sightings overall, as we embark upon a Second Cold War, we should expect the pattern to hold.

So far, this has been true—even down to the influence of balloons.

In February 2023, China announced that it was preparing to shoot down a UFO they had found in their skies (Rahman, 2023). The state-run newspaper *Global Times* said that such an object had been found near the city of Rizhao and that the government was urging fishermen to find safety in the event that the object may crash into or near the waters.

Earlier that month, the United States and Canada shot down three objects in their airspaces. However, one of these turned out to be nothing more—in relative terms—than a Chinese spy balloon.

This object had a moment of infamy when it was spotted coming from the Pacific and traveling across the continental United States. The balloon's purpose was to collect data on intelligence signals and was said to be part of a wider Chinese spy program.

Beijing, however, denied this. They insisted that it was merely a meteorological balloon that had flown off course. Furthermore, it was owned and supposedly operated by civilians.

The object was shot down over the Atlantic and recovered by military personnel.

But that was not all. In that same month, an object the size of a small car was shot down over Alaska. Another was shot down over the Yukon, Canadian Prime Minister Justin Trudeau confirmed. Despite taking place over Canadian airspace, this was performed by the USAF.

The reason for this, however, was simple: The object had begun its North American journey in Alaska and drifted into the Yukon. Trudeau and President Joe Biden had called one another and ordered the object shot down. Since it crashed in Canadian territory, Trudeau said Canadian Forces could collect the debris and begin studying it to determine its origin and purpose.

Were all of these objects part of a Chinese campaign to spy on the United States and Canada? Are balloons making a return to the espionage game?

And what about the one found over China? Did it have its origins in the United States?

Or is something much more sinister going on?

To think about this more deeply, we should take a trip back in time and investigate the Xiaoshan Airport incident.

This occurred as far back as 2010. On July 7th, a UFO appeared over the airport and hovered there (ABC News, 2010). The object was detected by radar. Aviation authorities were alerted. Around eighteen flights had to be delayed or canceled since this object was, frankly, in the way.

The whole incident lasted an hour until the object left and normal flights could resume.

But what was it? The ABC News report quotes a man who allegedly took a picture of the craft, saying it was a bright light that streaked across the sky. The report is quick to admit, however, that the man may have taken a picture of something completely unrelated to the incident.

The report also quotes an internet user, a move characteristic of journalism in that decade. The internet user suggests that this must have been an American intelligence operation or perhaps an American bomber on its way to attack some other part of China.

Another internet user, the article says, suggests that the idea it was from the United States is preposterous, considering this would likely lead to a war between the two countries. More than likely, the user suggests, this was something the Chinese government made.

While it may be questionable for a new organization to use Twitter to gather quotes, the quotes are nonetheless illustrative of a pattern we have been noticing these past few chapters. Namely, that an event featuring a genuine unknown is interpreted using cultural and political terminology.

That the United States and China are spying on one another goes without saying. But in this case, the UFO over the airport was of an unknown origin, and, as of this writing, is of an unknown origin *still.* Despite this, the need to know and understand the information to categorize what does not fit led Twitter users to try and impose a definition on the event that used present-day concerns of increasing tensions between the United States and China.

But while it is interesting to note the ways in which culture and politics affect our understanding of the world, this does nothing to answer the question of what was in the skies over that airport.

Here, we can add an interesting wrinkle into the mix.

While much of the initial reporting focused on a number of alleged photos of the craft, the photos themselves may have a much more terrestrial origin. Several of them, in fact, are helicopters (Kurczy, 2010). Not only that, but a good number of them had been available on the internet for quite some time before they were associated with the airport UFO.

Interestingly, in 2006, O'Hare Airport in Chicago had a similarly disruptive UFO hover over it. However, while no investigation was conducted, and airport workers were told not to speak to the media, the press did not leap to the idea that the disruptive object was alien in origin. In fact, the *Tribune* stated that it could have been from any number of things (Kurczy, 2010, quoting *The Chicago Tribune*).

In other words, the difficulty in interpreting the event lies in whether our willingness to believe it came from another world is clouding our judgment. While it is not impossible that a UFO passed over the Xiaoshan Airport, it is also not impossible that it was a terrestrial object, perhaps a large balloon, that got stuck over the airport at night. Given the use of balloons as tools of spycraft, this may well be exactly what that was.

But how are we to know?

And why does this problem seem intent on never going away?

***

Yet again, we have very little to go on outside of some scattered eyewitness reports, some of which may be colored by the urge to have experienced something beyond imagination. But what we do have is the sheer persistence of this phenomenon and its unwillingness to be resolved.

As the Second Cold War heats up, it is likely that these encounters will not only continue but become more frequent. That was the case last time—and whether because of the modern use of balloons for spying or because our extraterrestrial companions have an active interest in the history of our world—perhaps even *influencing* it— we will surely see the pattern hold.

Only this time, as we saw in Tehran, and as we will soon see again, these crafts seem intent on no longer just appearing to one or two people. In fact, they seem hellbent on appearing to as many people as possible in the most public places.

Chapter 13:

The Phoenix Lights—Mass Sightings in the American Southwest

In 1997, Arizona Governor Fife Symington did the unthinkable.

Just a few months prior, Phoenix had been host to one of the most-seen UFO sightings in history (Duda, 2024). The press was hot with the story; people all over the United States were talking about it, and the pressure was on the governor to address what may have been, to some, the most significant event in the history of UFOlogy.

Additionally, the governor was in a bit of hot water. He had a number of scandals boiling around him, including ones related to fraud. How he handled this moment, his aides told him, might have an enormous impact on his reelection campaign.

So the governor did the unthinkable: He ordered a press conference. He stood behind a podium, allowing the moment to be broadcast on CNN, as well as all the other major news networks. He told the nation what had happened, what was happening, and what would happen.

Then, right in front of the cameras and the whole world, he brought an alien on stage.

The Phoenix Lights

Let's back up for a moment.

The world in 1997 was a very different one from today. Clinton was in the White House; Puff Daddy dominated the charts; Pierce Brosnan was still James Bond; and two powerhouse book franchises, the *Harry Potter* and *Jack Reacher* books, both began their histories, as the first of each was published by that year's end.

Perhaps more to the point, it was the twilight years after the Cold War and before 9/11. This was the time Francis Fukuyama famously declared "the end of history," when the battle for the soul of the world had been fought, and as it had been won by the world's democracies, that this type of liberal democracy would be the standard for the rest of time.

Is it strange, then, that UFO sightings should continue during this period? Every time we think we understand their motivations, we are wrong. They do not only appear interested in our superpowers or dangerous technology but appear in places and to people in such a way that it lends credence to the idea that perhaps their motivations are impossible to understand.

But at least we know they are trying to stay secret. This is why they do not reveal themselves—either because they are scared of how we may react to them or because they are manipulating us from behind the scenes, along with the shadowy elements of our government. In fact, since the incident in Tehran was a one-off, we can safely assume that an error had been made and maybe even that the whole thing was an accident. Likely, considering our inferiority to them, it was an accident on the part of some human government official, who was no doubt punished for his transgressions.

But if we think that is the case, then the Phoenix Lights incident should make us rethink everything we think we know about what is happening in our skies.

The incident itself happened, as we said, in 1997. Over the city of Phoenix, Arizona, there appeared a large, V-shaped object (KTAR.com, 2017). Its bottom was decorated with a number of lights, but its size was such that it struck terror into the hearts of Phoenicians all across the city.

Of its size, some estimates say that it was a mile from end to end. Perhaps it was this aspect of it more than anything that led some residents to declare it "otherworldly." It just hovered, totally silent, blocking out the stars with its enormous bulk.

Is this unusual for Phoenix? Certainly, the sheer size of the object makes it unique. Yet, Phoenix is host to the largest number of UFO sightings of any other city in America. The Lights incident, although terrifying to experience, has since become a source of municipal pride.

Because not only was it a gigantic object, whatever it was, it was seen by an astonishing number of people. This includes police officers, city officials, civilians—everybody who was anybody, it seems, bore witness to the bizarre craft that hovered over the Arizona night sky.

The governor himself said he saw the thing. In fact, he was the one who called it "otherworldly." He said further that, as a pilot, he had some experience with things in the sky. But this was not something he had ever encountered before.

At least, this was what he said *after* his press conference. What he said *at* the press conference was something else entirely.

The Press Conference

Governor Symington was in trouble.

At the time of the Lights incident, he was going to trial for bank fraud charges (Duda, 2024). The results of this trial, where he was found guilty and pardoned some years later, would be worthy of a book in itself. But for our purposes, it is only important to note that he was under a lot of pressure.

Once the Lights incident happened, that pressure included the suggestion that he address the people and tell them what had happened. After all, it appeared to some people that there was no longer any question regarding UFOs: they were not only real, they were here, and, despite their reputation for secrecy, they had appeared in front of an entire, major American city.

Symington elected to host a press conference, which would be broadcast to the nation. This, it seemed, would provide him with two opportunities at the same time: He could not only put people's fears to rest about the UFO, but he could perhaps gain some good press and maybe even the support of the people of Arizona. It was, in other words, the perfect time to get people to like him.

However, this did not go as planned.

When Symington appeared behind the podium to address the people, he said that, yes, the source of the lights had been found. Not only that, but it was right there in the room with them.

With that, he brought one of his aides up on stage. His aide, however, was dressed head-to-toe in an alien costume—one that featured big, black eyes, a huge head, a silver onesie, and long fingers that ended in big, black nails.

The idea was to make people laugh. But that did not work. Within a short time after the press conference, Symington was telling the country that he had not only seen the lights himself but that they appeared to be "otherworldly" (KTAR.com, 2017).

Why the one-eighty? For some people, the Phoenix Lights event was no laughing matter. Not only was it taken seriously by UFOlogists, but since the general public had bore witness to such a momentous occasion, it seemed that perhaps the seriousness of the subject should be reflected in the governor's response.

Whatever Symington's blasé attitude toward the event, it has since become a part of America's cultural mythology. So much so, in fact, that it crossed over into the life of one of America's great myth-makers.

Who Goes There?

American cinema is bursting at the seams with mythological figures. Especially in the action and western genres, actors like John Wayne, Arnold Schwarzenegger, Sylvester Stallone, and Clint Eastwood embody the values of the great nation, with their individualism, their stubbornness, their sense of being a part of something greater than themselves, and perhaps, also, their willingness to use violence when necessary.

Among these figures, the great Kurt Russell stands tall. A Disney actor from a young age, Kurt Russell went on to become a towering icon in action and horror with his roles in *The Thing*, *Escape From New York*, and *Tango & Cash*. To this day, he remains a strong, commanding presence on the screen and a patriotic American to his very core.

Fascinating, then, that the streams of American myth should cross—that Snake Pliskin should be present for a momentous event of another kind.

On March 13, 1997, Kurt Russel was flying a private airplane across Arizona (KTAR.com, 2017). The idea was to fly his son to visit his son's girlfriend, which, it seems for Russel, was not an occurrence of any special import.

However, as he approached the Phoenix airport, he found himself looking at a large, V-shaped cluster of lights hovering over the city. He thought this was strange, of course, and when he landed he reported what he had seen. But from there, he let the incident slip from his mind and did not think back to it.

Years later, while watching television with Goldie Hawn, a report on the Phoenix Lights came on. In it, it was claimed that the lights were first reported by a general aviation pilot—meaning, a civilian flying their own jet.

It was then that Kurt Russel realized it was him who had first reported the Phoenix Lights.

What Happened?

Kurt Russell's presence may provide an interesting parallel in terms of America's mythological and folkloric landscape, but the fundamental question is still on the table—much as it has been in every case we have examined so far.

What happened?

There are several theories we can dismiss immediately. For example, given the number of people who saw the object and the photos taken of it (which were not hoaxes), we can say quite conclusively that this was not a mass hallucination. Nor does it seem to have been subjected to the vagaries of memory: An object showed up, was seen by perhaps thousands of people, and then left. There are no versions of this where a creature descends from the object or any other fantastical additives that have colored some of our other cases.

Something entered Phoenician airspace. Something occupied space and remained over a period of time. It was something that could be seen, however dimly. Of the things it could be seen doing, we can include "hovering" and "moving."

What else do we have to go on? Certainly, the incident did not lead to an announcement that aliens do exist and visit us regularly, so we can assume that whatever investigation was undertaken did not lead to that revelation. But while, by this point, we should be used to this sequence of events, there is little doubt that the divergence between what the people say is happening and what the government says are in such sharp division that one can't but think that a resolution is due to occur sooner than later.

In fact, we might say that there is something "institutionalized" about the typical skeptical response (Pasulka, 2023). Even as belief in UFOs has become more mainstream, it still remains a kind of "outsider" discourse—meaning that it is undertaken by people largely outside the confines of the academy, media, and other major institutions.

This outsider discourse, which posits not only that UFOs exist but that they are piloted by aliens, exists as a kind of oral tradition within the United States, which then has been extended through social media. It bears little resemblance to the institutional narrative, which states that these are flares, the planet Venus, or the object of a mass hysteria. In fact, the folk claims on the topic tend to incorporate the idea that this narrative functions as a kind of conspiracy, turning it into a power move to keep the people more or less in their place.

There is something to this divergence between the two narratives that looks suspiciously like unbalanced power. Even as the people continue to discuss and share information, all while developing a unique folklore (or discovering the truth) about the phenomenon, they are, in a sense, written off as rubes who need to have the finer points of the empirical sciences given to them in the simplest form possible.

In a way, that may have been why Symington's joke did not go over so well. Beyond the fact that he was not taking the concerns of the people seriously, he was actively disparaging their interest in alien visitations. This is not to say that *every single thing* the people are concerned about deserves consideration. But it does say that dismissing their concerns as a joke does little but aggravate the people being spoken down to and maybe even exacerbates the sense that the powerful are having one kind of discourse at the expense of everyone else.

This bifurcation may be partially responsible for some of the more extreme elements of UFO folklore. As consideration around UFOs becomes more and more marginalized, and as the scientific community continues to denigrate the field, it is perhaps only natural that some of the claims among UFOlogists would become increasingly strange.

Here, we should examine the degree to which this has happened in some corners of UFOlogy.

Multiple Species Of Alien

In the chapter on the Zimbabwe school incident, we hinted at the belief among some UFO enthusiasts that various species of aliens exist and visit the Earth. While the public perception likely focuses on the Little Green Men or gray aliens, there are some who posit a wide variety of types and even a hierarchy among them, as well as which ones are on "our side" and which ones are our enemies.

Some of this information comes from alleged abductees, and some from people who worked—or claim to have worked—in the upper echelons of government (Salla, 2005). This information includes the possibility that there are aliens who visit the Earth but look exactly like us. These aliens, it is said, could be among us at this very moment—they could even be in the White House, and we would not know it.

Some of these aliens come from the Sirius A system, and some from Sirius B. The ones from Sirius B tend to be evil, and the ones from A tend to be more or less aligned with human interests—at least, non-elite human interests.

See, the ones from Sirius B gave our governments a terrible weapon. This is known as Montauk technology, which provides our governments with the ability to time travel. But more on that in a second.

Of the alien species we know about, the most common are the grays, but there are also the "tall whites," which first appeared in the Mojave desert and occasionally help us out. The grays are the ones who tend to abduct us and were first encountered at Roswell, and are, generally, considered hostile.

However, it is the reptilians who are the most frightening of all.

The stories about these beings are quite incredible. To begin with, it is said that they may be native to Earth and perhaps played a role in creating humans. (Here, the similarities to Lovecraft's *At The Mountains Of Madness* are striking.) It may also be that these are the beings we call Fallen Angels (demons), although that is disputed.

These are, however, only one *kind* of reptilian. There are also off-world reptilians who see humans as a species to be harvested and controlled since we are so much lesser than they are. They perpetrate horrific human rights abuses on us, all with the full participation of our governments.

Still, it is suggested that perhaps the reptilians—"the Dracs"—are taking orders from a *still* more powerful race that is, at present, unknown to us—no doubt this causal link could go on forever until one arrives at a godlike being.

But we should address the Montauk technology.

The Nordic aliens—Rigelians—had a civil war that led to some of them relocating to the planet Procyon (Salla, 2005). The ones who stayed on the planet Rigel, meanwhile, had a full-blown nuclear war, which, along with environmental collapse, led to them living under the ground. The ones at Procyon, meanwhile, found themselves subjected to abduction and experimentation by the grays, which suggests that the grays are a kind of interplanetary scourge of evil scientists.

To counter gray influence, the Procyons developed a method of time travel that the grays could not undergo, as something about their biology did not jive with the process. Then, once the Procyons discovered that we were being manipulated by this same scourge, they decided to help us and to do so, have provided us with this time travel technology.

Now, the Montauk technology is the evil version of this. This was given to our governments by the people of Sirius B and involves the ability to travel to various nodal points throughout history—say, the collapse of the Soviet Union—and *rewrite it* so that the outcome is to your benefit. The reptilians, the American government, all use it to travel through time and change history, making them not only our current tyrants, but our tyrants throughout the *entirety of history.*

The time machines given to us by the Procyons, then, are not only crucial for fighting back against the grays; they are the very key to our survival: Without them, there is quite literally nothing we can do to fight back.

So much for the hierarchy and their weapons of domination. With that, we should return to the reptilians.

The reptilians were first brought to the public's attention through a book by David Icke titled *The Biggest Secret.* In it, he suggests that a number of high-profile celebrities, and especially government officials, are, in fact, members of a race of shape-shifting reptilian humanoids who have been controlling the world for thousands of years (Icke, 2000). In addition to this, they have a plan he calls a Global Agenda, which is, in effect, the creation of the perennial New World Order, a surveillance state with a centralized economy and no freedoms.

One of the most fascinating aspects of the book is that it implicates figures like Princess Diana, who he says was a threat to the Global Agenda and killed for it; George W. Bush and Henry Kissinger, who are working toward implementing the Global Agenda; and a number of manufactured crises in the forms of wars and terrorist attacks, which are designed to bring the Agenda into being.

The famous figures he brings into his narrative also may or may not be reptilians themselves. As he puts it, reptilians have a chameleonic ability that we might call "shape-shifting," meaning they can disguise themselves as human beings. (Although a discerning eye will be able to pick up on certain of their tells—the eyes, for example, that refuse to remain human.)

In essence, while the book is renowned for its lunacy, it is nonetheless a riveting entry into the creation of modern mythology. It has the good vs. evil struggle that we can find in many of the world's religions; it has the element borrowed from Gnosticism that gaining the forbidden knowledge will set you free; and it promises a Heaven On Earth, so long as enough of the elect can manage to overthrow their reptilian overlords and finally create paradise.

Perhaps it is for this reason that we have elected to discuss it in the context of the Phoenix Lights.

The High Cost Of No Interest

Icke's book was published only two years after the Phoenix Lights. This fact is crucial for understanding the state of UFO research at the time, as it had devolved into an elaborate and deeply paranoid mythological system.

While there are many reasons for this, one of them is the sheer amount of ridicule that was directed toward what was an empirical question: Are these things [UFOs] real? More to the point, the fact that so many people could bear witness to them at once, all with the same—or similar—story and that now it could be *photographed by many different people*, should have indicated that there was something there that was worth studying. In the absence of it being taken seriously, and maybe also because of the insistence that this was not a scientific problem, it was only natural that the phenomenon would take on the characteristics of a religion.

This was not a problem that was ready to go away, or even become more manageable. Because as we noted, this event, the Phoenix Lights, was captured by several cameras, leaving the possibility of it being a hoax, or hysteria, in the dust.

As technology, especially photographic and video technology, got better, and more accessible, the public would only become more and more privy to the types of things happening in the air all the time.

Sooner or later, they would want answers.

Chapter 14:

Technology and Truth—The Role of Modern Media in UFOlogy

Over the past few years, the types of accessible technology—"accessible" meaning "available for personal use"—have made an enormous leap forward. In a sense, this is inevitable with technology as a whole, but especially when it is under pressure. We might think of it as a sort of evolution, where if there is a need for technology to evolve, research and development will zero in on it to bring that tech into existence at the cheapest price it can.

This evolutionary trajectory of technology has led us to the development of rockets, mRNA vaccines, CRSPR gene-editing and cybernetics. It has made us smarter, helped us live longer, and better understand, to some extent, the world around us. Its implications look toward a future that is both liberating and horrifying.

The past fifteen years or so have seen old media formats upended in the face of a slew of decentralized digital apparatuses. Without oversight, this has led to a proliferation of information that would have previously been inaccessible to us—as well as a flood of made-up, manufactured, deepfaked fictions so believable in their presentation that it is often impossible to tell the difference.

That this has created a challenging political landscape is common knowledge by now. The fact that the president's voice and image can be deepfaked provides ample opportunity for chaos agents to make our lives quite miserable indeed. This is true even as it allows us to watch news developments in real time, keep a better eye on our leaders, and increase levels of accountability more than ever before.

It is as ambiguous a development as any we can imagine. Technology has brought truth and fiction into a catastrophic collision, and in such a way that few of us, if any, have any idea how to navigate it.

Already, the UFO phenomenon is fraught with ambiguity. Images of alleged crafts have been outed as hoaxes; videos of alien autopsies broadcast on television, only to be outed as hoaxes themselves; and yet all the while, we have videos, testimony, medical evidence, an increasingly large pile of evidence, all suggesting that perhaps, beyond the hoaxes, there is something real, something tangible to this phenomenon.

How can technology do anything except make this problem worse? How can it not distort the truth to such an extent that the truth itself becomes impossible?

In an age of an increasing mixture of fact and fiction, what will be the fate of UFOs?

Evolution

The original digital cameras captured images by focusing light on a sensor; then, this information—the light—would be converted into a digital image. Recently, however, this method of capturing images has become all but obsolete, as camera technology utilizes new methods for capturing the most detailed image possible.

One of the most innovative ways for doing this involves the use of algorithms to sort visual data into an image (Gupta, 2021). In essence, the conversion of raw light data into an image is done computationally, which is why our cell phones, despite their size and price, are able to take such good-quality pictures.

But the most fascinating thing about this is that it has implications not just for camera technology but for other things as well. This includes augmented reality and robotics but could also help in the development of self-driving cars and space exploration.

Perhaps the most advanced type of camera technology in existence is one that can capture images at the level of individual photons. This is still in its developmental stage, but the idea is that these cameras image at a trillion frames-per-second, can take images *from around corners*, and even detect images in what appears, to us, to be total darkness.

Taking images from around corners has an obvious angle with military and policing, as it would eliminate the possibility of being surprised by something on the other side of a building. It could theoretically be used to get a look inside of, say, caves, where it would have been too challenging to get a person inside, and too expensive to use drones or R.C. devices.

The real problem this poses, however, is that once we have the ability to produce images at that level of quality, our ability to create digital (read: fake) versions of the same is increased. Deepfakes are a problem now, but there are still glitches and other tells that can tip you off to the truthfulness of the image or video. The more camera technology increases, in concert with CGI and other technologies, the more likely we are to wind up with videos so believable that there is no discernible way to tell if they are fake or not.

We all remember the famous incident where Orson Welles performed a radio version of *War Of The Worlds*. The effect that performance had on listeners has been exaggerated over time, but there were still those who were panicked by its apparent veracity.

How will we react when we are provided with a detailed, convincing video of Washington, D.C., being overrun by insectoid aliens from the Crab Nebula?

The Big One

If the launch of the internet was a game-changing moment, it was not clear to what extent it would be so. Certainly, people wondered aloud about the possibilities, and many of them waxed utopian about what it would bring us. But the form the internet took and how it influenced and shaped us and our culture was impossible to predict.

One of the ways the internet has changed our social landscape is in how it has given us the ability to create media. Every minute, 100 minutes of content is uploaded to YouTube (Hirshberg, n.d.). This content consists of a wide variety of things, including music, podcasts, sketches, short films, and news commentary. But with the launch of one website, the whole media ecosystem received a jolt as we all gained the ability to become "content creators."

The addition of websites like Spotify and Twitter and apps like TikTok has given us a variety of media through which we can make the kind of content we want to make (or sell) and then use these platforms for distribution *for free*. In fact, if we do well on them, we can wind up in a revenue-sharing agreement that makes both us and the company quite rich.

The downsides to this are legendary. As everyone suddenly became responsible for their own "brand" and "media empire," lots of responsibilities were placed in their laps that many of them did not see coming. In fact, it soon became apparent that these media were having an outsized effect on the real world, particularly as they reinforced certain thought patterns we were already susceptible to.

For example, the Boston Marathon bombing. After the incident, the FBI released a series of photographs, each representing a suspect. The public was encouraged to keep an eye out for these men and to report them if they were seen.

Meanwhile, a young man named Sunil Tipathi's photo was uploaded to Facebook, as he was reported missing. In addition to being missing, however, Sunil suffered the unfortunate fate of looking like one of the suspects—so much so that someone uploaded Sunil's picture to Reddit, saying that this was the man they were all looking for.

At this time, Buzzfeed was still a popular destination for internet users. Once it got a hold of the picture and the boy's name, they ran with it, publishing an article claiming that, yes, this was, in fact, the Boston marathon bomber. Not only that, but it tweeted this information out to its 100,000 followers.

This led to a number of internet Twitter and Reddit users tracking down Sunil's family. Once they got a hold of the family's phone number, they barraged the family with phone calls, many of them containing death threats and the use of racial epithets.

Despite this, people continued to make media out of the story. It was a way to gain traction on Twitter, YouTube, or Reddit, and all without thinking of what kind of effect this was having on real people.

Once the truth came out that Sunil was not the Boston marathon bomber, it was true that some Reddit users were contrite. They used the opportunity to reflect on what they had done and how this had impacted people in the real world. One of them said he hoped that this would be the moment that people realized the kind of power they wield by helping control and create information on a site like Reddit.

Since then, our ability to surround ourselves with information that confirms our pre-existing views has only increased. While there are efforts to make people more aware of just how powerful a tool the internet can be, there are still instances all the time when the internet's power is misused, and someone's life is destroyed as a result.

In other words, if we are becoming more sensitive to the power we have at our disposal, we are doing very little to show it.

The 2010s also saw a rise in television using its powers for ill. While film and television have never been shy about trying to get eyes on screens by any means necessary, a number of cases throughout that decade revealed a newfound interest in promoting pseudoscience as a means of doing so.

For example, the History Channel has become a kind of repository for less-than-scientific programming (Schiele, 2020). Even *Shark Week* has gone from living up to its title and featuring programming about sharks to featuring shows about conspiracies to cover up the current existence of the megalodon.

The Curse of Oak Island is another of these, in which a group of reality contestants search for a legendary treasure supposedly buried in Nova Scotia. Of course, they found nothing—but that did not stop the producers from coming back the next year, and the next, and the next, to find increasingly esoteric objects. This included, at one point, Shakespeare's original manuscripts and even the Holy Grail.

Of course, people can enjoy programming without believing it is true, and we can be charitable enough to say that this is likely the case here. Television, like any entertainment medium, is subject to the profit motive, which means it gives people what they want. The question then, however, is how it comes to be that people want these things in the first place.

Perhaps we need look no further than the internet. This is where we all congregate, seeking out like-minded people and surrounding ourselves with information that tells us we were right along and those *other* people are the ones who are crazy, immoral, or dangerous. Once these ideas become solidified, and TV producers notice this, it is only natural that they provide us with programming that, just like the internet, tells us we were always right to believe in whatever strange thing we have always believed in.

Paranormal Predictor

Do programs about the paranormal convince people that the paranormal is real? Or do people consume media about the paranormal because they already believe in it?

One recent study found that a person's belief in the paranormal could be predicted based on the media they consume (Stise et al., 2023). Specifically, they found that someone who watched Fox News, listened to *The Joe Rogan Experience*, used YouTube regularly, and watched documentaries on the paranormal was more likely to believe that the paranormal was real. (Here, we can understand the paranormal in the broadest sense.)

It is an interesting study but does not answer the question we began this section with. In a way, it is like saying that you can predict someone's interest in World War II by whether or not they watch documentaries on the subject. But unless you go into their life story, you cannot know with that information alone whether or not those documentaries *gave* that person an interest in WWII, and even then, you cannot know all the influences previous to that moment that primed this person to be convinced by a documentary.

That said, we might be able to assume a reciprocal relationship between the two in the following way: We create media, meaning we create the kinds of things we are interested in seeing; we take in the media of others, which they create for us in order to be seeing (i.e., playing to our pre-existing interests); and the media we take in reinforces certain pre-existing interests, to the extent that it amplifies them.

This is only an idea. But if it is true, then the question of whether we are being "programmed" by our media or are merely taking in things we want to see is irrelevant: Media reveals to us who we really are and, in doing so, makes us more of that thing.

UFO

What does this have to do with the UFO subject?

Let's take a small step back to where we were in the last chapter. By then—in fact, long before then—a pattern had emerged with the UFO story.

First, there would be the initial encounter; sometimes, this was captured via photograph, but oftentimes, especially before the wide availability of that technology, it was not. The person or persons who had this encounter would report it, which usually led to some interest on the part of an authority or a reporter. After that, more people would report on either the same exact experience or else they would have an experience of their own that was just too similar for it to be a coincidence. In cases where a number of UFO sightings occurred over a period, the number of individual cases may be extremely high; in cases where there was only one or a couple, there would be more evidence, usually conflicting evidence, that would make the case more difficult.

Eventually, an investigation would ensue. This was usually because of public pressure or genuine concern about, say, a dangerous technological advance. The investigation would find a number of alarming things, usually by talking to witnesses, who, more often than not, seemed reliable.

However, the investigation would ultimately yield nothing. Most of the reports would turn out to be bunk, and the ones that could not be disproven could not be tested since they were a unique-ish occurrence. Once the investigation stalled, it would usually be revealed that there was nothing going on, and everyone could move on to the next thing.

Every time. Even as cases became more challenging to dismiss, like some of the ones from Belgium, the one in Tehran, and the one in Phoenix, the pattern held. These were encounters that may have had multiple independent witnesses or photographic evidence, but still, they were dismissed, even ridiculed.

Technology has altered the playing field. We do not need to rely on government investigations, incredulous journalists, or scientists who think the whole thing is crazy or stupid. We can take high-quality images ourselves, and if we have a good one, we can just publish it on Twitter.

The gatekeepers have left the building, and the inmates have taken over the asylum. But this double-edged sword can either bring out the truth of the UFO phenomenon or bury it forever.

Faked videos and photos will no doubt be more common. But more than that, the internet is a breeding ground for rumors and falsehoods. A misinterpretation of a helicopter in a video at night can find itself turned into a video *revealing the true nature of the alien conspiracy.*

In a field already fraught with hoaxes, deception, false memories, and instances of genuine psychosis—relying on experts is not necessarily a bad thing. Remember, David Icke wrote about the reptilian humanoids before the widespread adoption of the internet.

Imagine what strange horrors are awaiting us when we publish our high-quality UFO photos to an echo chamber primed to concoct the strangest possible interpretation of it.

The Bad News

Now that video and camera technology have become so advanced, the standards for what counts as an acceptable UFO report have changed with it.

The reasoning for this is simple: In previous years and decades, when someone would take a video of a supposed UFO, the end product would be grainy, its details difficult to make out. There was no way of knowing whether the thing you were seeing was a helicopter, a plane, or, sometimes, the glow of some strategically placed electric lanterns in the woods. Because of this, it would require careful interpretation, as well as much arguing. It would feed into, and off of, the polarization between believers and skeptics, with each group certain that the video proves their suspicions.

But imagine for a moment that we had an iPhone-quality camera during the Belgian wave. If we had, we could expect two things: First, *there would be video*—there is just no way, with how accessible the phone is (in our pockets), that nobody would have made an attempt at filming the UFOs that plagued Belgium during those few years.

Secondly, and most importantly, the videos would have been clear and detailed. There would have been little doubt about what we were looking at because these devices, through the built-in algorithms, can sort raw light data into photos and videos that are, in some cases, more detailed than what our eyes can make out, especially during the night.

In the present, then, the effect is manifold. For starters, since we have access to this technology and can produce these types of videos, there is no more room for hearsay or anecdotal reports. We can no longer place any interest in the testimonies of people who encountered flying objects in the woods *unless that testimony is accompanied by video.*

The reason for this is simple: We have the means with which to record our experiences. All of us. If someone who was in possession of one of these phone cameras saw a UFO and refused to document it, their testimony should be considered suspect.

This means, too, that in journalism, anecdotal stories should no longer carry any water. The standard for what counts as a UFO story has shifted and now requires detailed, high-quality videos. That is good for journalism, on the one hand, since having such a high-quality video means possessing proof of UFOs, which would be, obviously, a good story. It is also bad for journalism since the clickbait, tabloid-style UFO story is no longer viable. It is not even believable.

All of which, in closing, should force us to ask one more, quite difficult question: If we can take such high-quality videos of UFOs, why have we not done so yet?

Where is the video proof that we are being visited by aliens?

Chapter 15:

Official Disclosure? Governments, Whistle-Blowers, and the Unveiling of Secrets

Deny. Deny. Deny.

Such was the playbook on UFOs. Investigations were stalled or obfuscated, UFOlogists were labeled as cranks or crazies, and the UFOs themselves were constantly written off as birds, stars, or hoaxes.

But there was only so long this could have gone on for. Eventually, there would be a break in the dam, and the water would come rushing through. In the ensuing flood, perhaps we would all ask ourselves why they kept telling us there was never any water on the other side.

Over the past few years, this is precisely what has happened. Where it all leads, we do not know yet—we are still in the middle of it all. But the path to disclosure has been hard-fought and at great reputational risk to everyone involved. It has meant an enormous number of people applying consistent pressure until finally the narrative took a turn that allowed even the skeptics to pause and think for a moment.

What if the subject is not related to the paranormal at all? What if this is a genuine scientific problem?

And what if its answers are relevant to the question of national security?

This is the story of the people who stuck their neck out to get somebody in charge to admit that something was going on. It is the story of reporters, activists, government workers, and military personnel who finally got the conversation out to the public and made incredible leaps in terms of re-contextualizing it as a subject worthy of our consideration.

In essence, it is the time when the pattern no longer holds, and finally, after decades of work, the investigation does not just fade away into nothingness.

Grusch

In 2023, David Grusch made a speech that would shock millions.

Speaking before the House Oversight Committee, he announced that, as a former intelligence officer, he had been privy to information about the government's relationship with UFOs (Grusch, n.d.). He said that not only was the government—specifically, the military—in possession of alien artifacts but that it had been for some time. More to the point, it had been covering up its involvement with alien technology and, in doing so, had made Grusch complicit in keeping secrets from the public—secrets which the public had an active interest in.

His reasons for coming forward with this information came from several motivations. To begin with, he said that he was on the side of truth and transparency and so intended to live up to these principles. He also understood that humanity could benefit from this information becoming public.

In essence, he saw progress could be made in the fields of technology and international relations if we came to recognize that we are not alone and have access to tech that could bring about incredible advancements in, say, space exploration. The *Star Trek*-type of future, he implied, was possible if only we came to terms with the truth about our place in the universe.

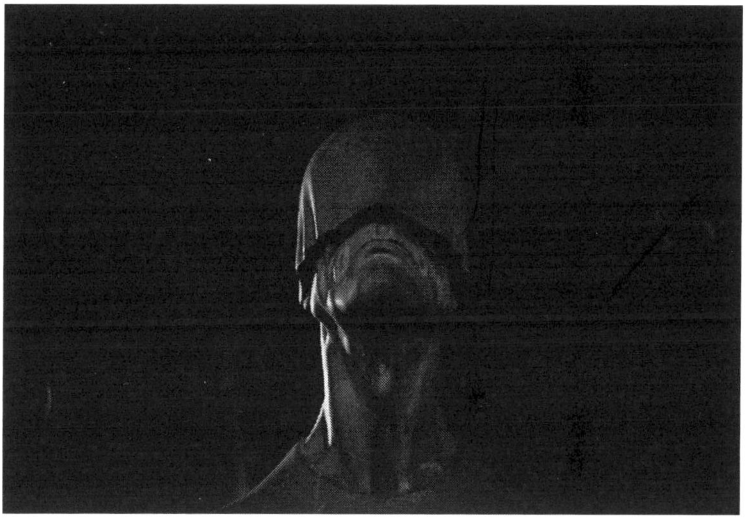

To say that this was an explosive revelation would be an understatement. It was reported on by every major publication in the United States, from the *Washington Post* to *AP News*. It was reported on by Canada's public broadcaster, the *CBC*, as well as *Al Jazeera*.

Virtually everyone shivered with excitement. Finally, someone with authority said it out loud: We are not alone; they have been here a long time, and we have been lying to you about it for decades.

But how did we get here? What were the incremental steps that led to this revelation? And just what does it all mean?

Legitimizing

There is little sense in rehashing the history of UFO research at this point. But what does need to be pointed out is that in between the time that UFO research went "underground" and when Grusch spoke in front of congress, there were a number of micro-movements that chipped away at the notion that UFOs were a topic of the paranormal, and not one of the sciences.

The first of these revolves around the question of whether intelligent life *might* exist on other worlds. Since the Victorian Age, scientists have gone back and forth on whether or not this is likely true (Lomas, 2024). One textbook from that period, in fact, says flat-out that for inhabitants on Mars, Earth must look larger compared to how Mars looks to us. In other words, they took it for granted that not only was there life on other worlds but almost certainly on the world next to ours.

At some point, this went out of fashion. Part of the reason for this came from the idea that planets themselves were relatively rare, which made the idea of a galaxy teeming with life almost impossible. But since 1995, when the first exoplanet was discovered, scientists have discovered *thousands* of planets in the Milky Way, leading NASA to estimate that there are perhaps 100 billion of them in our galaxy alone.

Our galaxy is, of course, one of two trillion in the observable universe. So the sheer number of planets that could be out there is literally impossible to comprehend. However, how many of those can sustain life is another question.

Thus enters what is called the "Goldilocks zone." This refers to a planet's "just right" distance from its sun, such that it is neither too hot nor too cold. Since relatively few planets fall into this category, it certainly reduces the total number of planets that could harbor life down to significantly fewer.

Yet, significantly fewer than 100 billion is still an enormous number. In fact, it might be the case that *every single star has at least one planet in the Goldilocks zone.*

Of course, that does not mean that every single one of those planets *can* support life. There are atmospheric conditions that are essential to this, such that life can take in, say, oxygen, in order to survive. It also has to be the kind of atmosphere that does not burn every life form that comes into contact with it, like the atmosphere on Venus.

So the number has gotten smaller still. It is still possibly quite large, but it is much smaller than it was in the beginning.

Then there is another layer of complexity: Our own planet has been host to an impossibly large number of lifeforms in its four billion years of life. Of all of those lifeforms, only one of them has ever been intelligent enough to build spaceships. So even if every star in the galaxy did have at least one planet that was in the Goldilocks zone, and *even if* every one of those planets had the right atmospheric conditions to support life, what are the odds that that life is intelligent enough to become a space-faring species?

Some scientists have settled on what they think is a sensible number of planets in our galaxy that are host to intelligent, civilized life. That number, alas, is roughly a dozen—quite a far cry from the 100 billion planets we started off with.

But while this tiny number may seem to be cause for disappointment, that is not necessarily the case. A dozen planets mean a dozen chances for life to discover ways to travel the stars.

So it is that, yet again, we reach what appears to be an impasse: "Okay, but what if traveling between stars is impossible? What if there is just too much distance between them, such that no living thing can last a trip from one to the other unless it lives an abnormally long time?"

Yet again, we have what might be an answer. Recently, scientists have been experimenting with propulsion systems that can reach extraordinary speeds (Lomas, 2024). One of these is a rocket that uses nuclear fusion to travel around 500k MPH. Still another is a kind of "laser sail" that can accelerate to half the speed of light after around a decade of travel.

This latter method may not sound impressive—after all, ten years is a long time to reach any speed—but consider just how fast the speed of light is. It is the fastest thing in the known universe, and we can possibly reach half of its speed through nothing but our own ingenuity.

If the idea of piloting a ship for ten years sounds exhausting, remember that it is becoming simpler and simpler to use artificial intelligence for a variety of tasks—including driving. Giving an AI the ability to pilot such a spaceship would mean human input into that task would be minimal, freeing us up to do all sorts of other work aboard the ship.

The list of technological possibilities for solving the problem of space travel is enough to warrant their own separate study. But what is important for us here is that while we may have once considered the idea that life does not exist elsewhere but could come here despite all the obstacles trying to prevent them from doing so, as fanciful, our own developments have gradually brought this question into the mainstream.

What if it really *was* the case that the UFO phenomenon was a scientific question?

That the question was no longer fanciful meant a huge step forward in terms of learning the truth. But it would take something much more drastic, and more punk rock, to really kick the doors open.

Tom DeLonge

In a development nobody saw coming, the story of UFO disclosure cannot be discussed without mentioning the name Tom DeLonge.

For millions of people, that name only ever meant one thing: blink-182. One of the most successful bands of the late '90s and early '00s, and certainly the most influential, blink-182 became famous not just for their unique combination of melancholic-yet-jumped-up pop songs about breakups, divorce, and the quest for maturity but for their telltale juvenile humor. For example, their live album *The Mark, Tom And Travis Show*, showcases the band's banter in between songs, often featuring jokes about sex, bodily functions, and a number of other scatological subjects. And more than one song featured lyrics that would make even the most hardened potty humor advocates blush.

Then, in 2017, DeLonge leaked three videos of UFOs, all of which were recorded using infrared cameras, and all of them filmed by the U.S. Navy (KCAL News, 2020). He did this through a private company of his, called To The Stars, which specializes in various "fringe" studies, among them the study of UFOs and the existence of alien life on Earth.

The videos themselves were later confirmed to be accurate by the Pentagon, who re-released the videos themselves. This was done, in part, to clear up any misconceptions about them, as well as to confirm that what was in the videos was not sensitive in a national security sense.

After this, the Navy released guidelines for its service members, regarding how to report on UFO activity. One of the pilots, whose jet had taken one of the videos in question, surfaced to comment on the nature of the incident.

As he told the story, the object was one he could not identify, and so made pursuit of it. As he did, it made some wild maneuvers of a kind that left him perplexed. He said that it was almost like a ping pong ball, the way it bounced from one side to the other.

This incident also led to the revelation that, between 2007 and 2012, the Pentagon had opened *yet another* program to study UFOs, which had begun because, yet again, the government had decided that these objects may be a national security concern.

Then, as all this was coming out, the former head of this program, Luis Elizondo, spoke to CNN about the program and about his experiences studying UFOs.

He said, in his opinion, that there is a very high probability that we are not alone.

Other government figures suddenly felt emboldened to come forward about their experiences also. One of them said that he was glad the videos had come out but that these only scratched the surface of what the government was in possession of. There were almost certainly aircraft-like objects that could make maneuvers beyond what the military was capable of, and no other country seemed to have these capabilities either.

Something appeared to be unfurling, which had been coiled up and concealed before.

Tom DeLonge may have ushered in a new era of openness about UFOs. Suddenly, it was all anyone could talk about.

Congressional Hearings

All of a sudden, pressure was put on the government to open up some more about the nature of their involvement with UFOs. If the Navy videos were real, and, as members of the government said, there was a whole lot more evidence than just that, then it seemed imperative that the government finally come clean and lay that evidence out for the people.

This culminated in one of the most widely-discussed Congressional hearings in quite some time. Three veterans were brought forward, each claiming to have information pertinent to the investigation (Romo & Chappell, 2023). If what they told was true, they did not disappoint.

Retired Maj. David Grusch, in particular, arrived with some stories that all but shook the entire nature. In his version of events, he was part of a program at the Pentagon to study UAPs (the new term for UFOs), and in doing so, interviewed dozens of people within the government who claimed they personally had seen not only alien technology but "biologics," implied to mean the bodies (living or dead) of alien beings.

He also claimed that these data—including photographs, oral testimony, and more—had been intentionally kept from Congress and that, in coming forward, he had been threatened by various government figures who wanted to keep him quiet.

Beyond Grusch, there were the testimonies of former Navy fighter pilot Ryan Graves and retired Cmdr. David Fravor. Each of them said that they had encountered UAP in the skies and described the bizarre shapes of these things as best they could.

Crucially, Graves said that UFO encounters were "neither isolated nor rare" (Romo & Chappell, 2023).

The reactions from members of congress are crucial to note as well. When Grusch said that the government possessed "biologics," there was an audible gasp. The same occurred when he said that he'd been threatened before coming to testify.

Democratic Rep. Robert Garcia of California, after the hearing, was quoted as saying that whatever these things are in the skies, they may pose a threat to national security. This means that there should be more reporting on them, not less, so as to bring more information out into the open.

The stigma, it appeared, had been lifted from UFOlogy. It was no longer the kind of thing you had to be ashamed of or admit to being interested in to people who would not laugh you out of the room. It was something the public took seriously, and more than that, something the government took seriously.

So what did everyone do about it?

The Results

One more time, with feeling.

In 2022, the Pentagon opened an office called the AARO, or All-domain Anomaly Research Office, to study UFOs—

specifically in response to the claims made by Navy and Air Force personnel (Tingley, 2024).

After nearly two years of collecting evidence, they found that there was no evidence that UFOs were extraterrestrials. The videos that had been circulated could all be explained as terrestrial phenomena, including—you guessed it—balloons.

Furthermore, AARO investigated the possibility that the Pentagon possessed alien technology or that they had been reverse-engineering alien technology. They found no evidence that this was true. In fact, as they put it, the idea that such a thing *was* true was due to circular reporting, meaning that people had told people who had told people, who had eventually told Grusch.

As a result, accusations have been made that AARO is perhaps a part of the coverup instead of the view through which we learn the truth. However, no empirical evidence has been found to support this, except that AARO failed to produce the kind of finding some people were primed to believe was true.

So here we have another group of sightings, leading to another military program to study them, explaining to us that these encounters were nothing more than satellites, technological glitches, and, yes, balloons.

Meanwhile, it will not be surprising to learn that despite all this, reports are still coming in from the Navy and Air Force regarding objects making strange maneuvers in the sky—things that cannot be from this Earth since nothing on Earth can perform these tasks.

Some critics of these findings have suggested that perhaps the people who had really seen UFOs did not trust AARO and so declined to speak with them. Therefore, AARO was only given the false stories, which proved the skeptics right. The *real* UFO stories are still out there, hiding on the margins.

But as the AARO report says, UAP tends to arise in the United States during times where people are worried about national security, or about technology in the broadest sense. The Cold War saw an uptick in sightings for this reason, and so, we here in the Second Cold War have seen the same.

The implication here is that the phenomena are projections of our fears. We see the thing that we are most scared of *because we are so scared of it.* "Aliens" were once communists; perhaps now they are the Chinese totalitarians or the Russian oligarchs. We have all been told about technological intrusions into our electoral processes, and we are more aware all the time of how Russian bots clog up our social media feeds with propaganda. What better metaphor for these things than alien outsiders crossing our borders with fearsome, unknowable technology?

***

The UFO story is fractal in structure. It is an infinite series of identical narratives, each nested in and producing the next one. There is no limit to how far you can go or how deep the structure is. There are an infinite number of narratives, differentiated only by the decade in which they occur.

This will not be the end because there are always more stories to find, more people who have seen the real thing, and more evidence that these things are out there.

Whether they are or not is perhaps beside the point. But by now, the expectation that the next time will be the time is beginning to sound like wishful thinking.

Chapter 16:

Cosmic Cultures—How UFOs Have Shaped the Human Experience

No matter what we try to do about it and no matter the information that gets fed back to us, aliens are a constant source of inspiration. They are our imaginary companions, propping up in fiction, religion, and life, perhaps to represent the things we most fear or the things we most desire. They are the perennial "other," always outside the margins, sometimes like us, sometimes not like us at all.

In science fiction especially, we have encountered aliens of an unthinkable variety. We have seen and been enthralled by the adventures of Spock, Chewbacca, and Dejah Thoris, or been assaulted and terrified by the xenomorph, the Predator, and, horror of all horrors, the dreaded Cthulhu. These aliens have been shapeshifters, humanoids, insects, or, like Lovecraft's more fantastical entities, literally beyond description.

We have also seen cults and religious movements spring up around them. Scientology is probably the most famous religion that incorporates alien beings, but there are still other, more obscure ones, with elaborate myths and, sometimes, even the promise of the believers being taken up into the sky with their alien saviors.

Especially over the past hundred or so years, our culture has been inextricably linked to the concept of alien life. It has not only imagined its possibilities but has also used it to help us make sense of our own.

Even if the results are sometimes disconcerting.

Gilgamesh

When we think of science fiction, we may think of several related tropes, like robots, the quest for knowledge, and various gadgets and weapons, like ray guns or faster-than-light travel. However, perhaps one of the most widely recognized storytelling tropes in the genre is the "traveling to another world" plot.

Star Trek is probably the most recognizable example of this. The characters in that show usually wind up on a new planet every episode, where they encounter some problem that they are not supposed to interfere with, only to interfere with it and wind up making things better.

This structure is most obviously borrowed from Homer's epic *The Odyssey*. But the idea of traveling between worlds is much more ancient than even Homer.

In fact, our oldest recorded story, *The Epic Of Gilgamesh*, is precisely that: A story of a man traveling from world to world. Like in *Star Trek*, what Gilgamesh seeks is knowledge.

The type of knowledge Gilgamesh seeks is immortality. To obtain the secret to unending life, he goes to all sorts of fantastical places, including, like Odysseus, the Underworld. Along the way, he encounters gods and monsters and learns the hard way, like Victor Frankenstein, that there are areas in which man was not meant to go. He recognizes his own limitations and the importance of a legacy of deeds as a kind of immortality, which allows him to come to terms with the fact of his impermanence in the world.

Here, we have several of the seeds for what would become science fiction. But for our purposes, the important one is that Gilgamesh travels to worlds that are "alien" to his own, where he encounters beings that are not like the ones he knows in his home of Babylon.

Even four thousand years ago, we were thinking about alien lands and the creatures we might find there.

Science Fiction

Once we move through the history of literature and land in science fiction proper, we find some controversy about where exactly this genre starts. *Frankenstein* is often considered the first, but some of Voltaire's works from earlier than that are considered examples of proto-science fiction.

However, *Frankenstein* aside, the first writers who wrote what we could recognize as being science fiction would be Jules Verne and H.G. Wells. We discussed these writers in an earlier chapter, and here we need to point out two things: Verne's book *From The Earth To The Moon* featured the first literary example of a machine that took people to a celestial body that was not Earth, and *War Of The Worlds* is the first story of an alien invasion.

The influence these two works had is incalculable. From them—and others by the same author—we wind up with the pulp era of science fiction, which was characterized by fast, action-based plots, often featuring rockets and aliens as adversaries or love interests. Here, the prototypical example is *The Princess Of Mars* by Edgar Rice Burroughs.

This gets interesting when we arrive at what is known as the Golden Age of science fiction. This era produced some of the field's most legendary writers, from Isaac Asimov, Robert Heinlein, and Arthur C. Clarke to lesser-known ones like A.E. van Vogt, Olaf Stapleton, and the inimitable Theodore Sturgeon. It was the era when science fiction "grew up," and many of the writers in the field then were scientists in their own right. For example, Asimov spent much of his life as a chemistry professor.

As science fiction grew up, so did its depictions of alien life. Edgar Rice Burroughs, for all his exciting plots and wild action, still depicted aliens as either fully or partially humanoid. But in works like *2001: A Space Odyssey*, we could see evidence of a new conception of alien life being brought into the popular consciousness—something so far removed from our understanding of the reality that it was beyond description.

In doing so, Arthur Clarke was no doubt drawing on the works of H.P. Lovecraft, with his completely alien life forms. However, if Lovecraft tended to focus on strange, tentacled beings with numerous eyes to represent alienness, in *2001*, the aliens themselves were so outside of comprehension that they never even came on stage. They were only known by their mysterious monoliths, through which they guided human evolution, from giving us the minds with which to wield tools, and finally, in the end, turning us into gods. It was as if the boundless dimension of imagination had become a stand-in for what was, ultimately, unknowable.

This tension between humanoid creatures and creatures utterly alien in every way has set the standard for depiction in sci-fi ever since. *Star Trek* famously depicts a galaxy populated with humanoid aliens and even explains it by saying that all of these species descend from the same ancestor. Films like *Arrival*, meanwhile, depict aliens that look almost like a bonier version of Thing from *The Addams Family* but with a gothic statue on top. They are hidden in shadow and fog, communicate by making shapes, and resemble only in very small ways what we would think of as human.

Interesting, then, how, in the UFO reports we have discussed, the ineffable alien never makes an appearance. Our contactees discussed everything from the gray aliens, to Nordics to reptilian humanoids—but never did any of them report an encounter with something that was utterly beyond comprehension.

Here, the movie *Mars Attacks!* might be pertinent. In it, the Martians are short, wear helmets, and have faces where the bottom looks skeletal and the top houses a large and exposed brain. They pilot spaceships that look like popular culture's understanding of a UFO, wield ray guns that turn people into green skeletons, and even say, "We come in peace" (although this is a method for tricking us credulous humans).

Although this is intended as a cartoonish depiction of the kinds of aliens we might find in B-movies from the 50s (such as *Invasion Of The Saucer Men*), it is nonetheless much closer to the depiction of gray aliens we have found most often in discussions around the aliens who pilot these strange ships. Meaning that they are human enough to be recognizable but alien enough that we feel a sense of the uncanny when we look at them. They look like something trying to be us and not succeeding.

Here, we find ourselves in the midst of a "chicken or egg" argument: Why is it that the aliens we supposedly encounter in real life appear to us in forms that are recognizable—i.e., as we encounter them in a certain kind of science fiction? Is science fiction having an influence on our beliefs about alien life? Or does this influence run both ways?

This is not a question we can answer, particularly since we do not possess an alien specimen with which to compare our fiction. We only have stories—either the ones in science fiction or the ones in contactee reports.

What these creatures *represent* to us, however, is something we can indeed explore.

UFO Cults

Perhaps the most alarming development in our relationship with UFOs and alien life more broadly is how it manifests in the form of religious cults. But probably the most infamous of these was a group that called itself Heaven's Gate.

This group was run out of San Diego by two people who went by the names of Do and Ti (Robinson, 1997). They formed Heaven's Gate sometime in the 1970s after claiming they were alien beings who had taken on human form. They claimed further that, for believers, a UFO would eventually come and take them all away to a place of peace and happiness. (This is what is known as a "cargo cult," where the end times prophecy is that something will come and take them away.)

They handed out pamphlets and wound up recruiting enough members that, for a time, they were considered a major new religious movement in the United States. They relied on the work of H.G. Wells to inspire their stories of myth and renewal, as well as capitalizing on events like Roswell and supposedly alien-related locations like Area 51. They even watched and took seriously *The X-Files* and *Star Trek*.

By the mid-90s, they relied almost exclusively on the internet to gain followers and promote their message. They professed a belief that soon they would leave behind the human chrysalis when they reached The Evolutionary Level Above Human (TELAH). But more than that, they became dangerously obsessed with a coming celestial event, which, they said, would signal it was time to leave their "containers" ("bodies") behind.

This celestial event was a comet known as Hale-Bopp. During other periods in history, it has been noted as a harbinger of cosmic change—so perhaps, in some sense, it was inevitable that it would be considered as such by Heaven's Gate. But what Heaven's Gate did in response to the coming of this comet was to strike horror in the hearts of people all over the Western world.

On March 26, 1997, the bodies of the members of Heaven's Gate were found in varying stages of decomposition. This included some 21 women and 18 men between the ages of 26 and 72. They had died after ingesting a combination of barbiturates and vodka, which had been placed in applesauce. But while this was what incapacitated them, it was not what killed them.

After eating the applesauce, the members all submitted to suffocation via plastic bag. Each of them had been dressed in unisex uniforms, with purple shrouds over their heads. Many of the men had been castrated.

The media reaction to this was interesting. Some early reports attempted to blame the internet for what had happened, saying that perhaps these were people whose brains had been cooked by too much exposure to the weirder corners of the Net. This was a strange angle to take since suicide cults have obviously been with us for a very long time. But more than that, they appeared to have genuine—if bizarre—religious beliefs based on an association between "aliens" and "heaven."

Despite the morbid context, this is a fairly intuitive association. "Heaven" is often thought of as being "above," despite the deeper religious sense of it being "other," almost like another dimension. Perhaps this is because of an association between "up" and "better," but in any case, we need only look at baseball players who point up to the heavens to thank God for a grand slam to know that our instinct is to see heaven as being above.

Heaven's Gate's use of the cargo cult framework works well within this paradigm. They say that beings will come and take the elect away from Earth, which is below, to a new place, which is above. They will enter paradise, albeit this time literally in outer space.

From there, we return to something we discussed in the chapter on the Middle Ages, albeit in a slightly different form. For Heaven's Gate, aliens were, in a sense, angels. They were beings from paradise who would come and take the elect away from their earthly troubles. This association between "higher life forms" in a biological, technological sense and "higher life forms" in a more spiritual, metaphysical sense is an easy one to make. Adding to them the tasks we normally assign to gods and angels is perhaps only inevitable.

But that is only scratching at the surface of what these creatures mean to us.

What Does It All Mean?

One way we can understand the alien as a metaphor is to see it as representing the "Other." We have touched on this already, but it is worth repeating: When we think of aliens, especially in fiction, we can often interpret them as representing the kinds of people who are outside of our cultural sphere.

In the 1950s, there were a number of notable examples of movies that played with this notion. Some of these included *Invasion Of The Body Snatchers*, *It Came From Outer Space*, and *Invaders From Mars*, where the aliens were shown to mimic or hide themselves within human beings. Behind these human faces, then, were alien beings with secret motives, usually involving the conversion of the townspeople so that they, too, would become aliens.

These were barely disguised metaphors for the fear of communism prevalent at the time. Many people, judging by their media, thought—*knew*—that any of their neighbors could be a secret communist. They could be meeting at clandestine locations and plotting how to convert people to the Cause.

What better way to depict that in fiction than as body-snatched pod people?

Other instances in fiction include *The Man Who Fell To Earth*, which is about an alien trying to pass as a human being, which becomes a metaphor for the writer's alcoholism. (An alcoholic here is a kind of Other—someone who lives, so to speak, on the Other Side.) But maybe the greatest depiction of the alien as Other is in the film *District 9*.

In this movie, aliens accidentally land their ship in South Africa, after which they find themselves in a science-fiction version of apartheid. The film's plot revolves around one of the white characters becoming infected with a kind of virus that turns him into one of the alien creatures, forcing him to become marginalized.

This was a clear allegory to the horrors of South African apartheid, with the aliens standing in for the Black South Africans. It was, and remains, one of the more powerful depictions of alien otherness in the history of film and literature.

There are other qualities aliens symbolize in film and literature, also. Sometimes, they are used as a showcase of our own qualities, such as our constant need to drain ecosystems dry in *Independence Day*; or perhaps they can represent the horrifying inhumanness of the universe itself, as in Lovecraft's Cthulhu mythos.

But even as those are all examples from fiction, they do suggest how we might view alien beings as a part of the UFO phenomenon. What they represent for us, in other words, might be similar to what they mean in our fictional representations.

In fact, what we might say is this: The reason why *Invasion Of The Body Snatchers* worked so well as a representation of the communist other is because the Cold War had just gone into full swing, and there was a genuine fear that the Soviets might claim victory via insurgents from within. Given this fear, is it any wonder there was such an uptick in UFO sightings?

Aliens and their technology represented, albeit unconsciously, the fears that Americans had about the Russians and their bombs. Notice, however, that this is true, in a way, whether or not there really are aliens and UFOs in America: Even if someone saw an actual alien in 1955, there would be a part of them that would understand the alien as being a threatening other, possibly with motivations not unlike those of the Soviets.

Of course, that is how we see them in times of turmoil. Heaven's Gate, despite ultimately being an expression of our worst, most horrific impulses, saw in the alien the potential for transcendence. The members literally wanted to leave their bodies, their human bodies, to become like something else. The body was a symbol of the spiritual state, with the human body being a kind of fallenness and the alien body being a kind of purified form.

Ultimately, the thread that holds it all together is that in the alien we see something *else*. Whether that is a part of us that we would rather remain hidden (for example, the psychosexual oral rape trauma of the xenomorph in *Alien*), or people whose way of life threatens ours, or our aspirations for the future, the alien is always something other than who we are now, or what our lives are at this moment.

Positive or negative, they are always the other thing.

But what, ultimately, does that tell us about who we are?

Cosmic Perspective

The gift and the curse of imagination is that it allows us to think outside of the present. We are not completely immersed in the needs of the moment—food, water, sex—but can compare ourselves to how things were in the past and imagine future scenarios that are, sometimes, radically different from our own.

But more than that, imagination can allow us to take an enormously transcendent step outside of ourselves so that we can tap on infinity's door. This might sound esoteric and strange, but it is in some sense the essence of mystical experience—to have "seen" the big picture, the world as it is outside of oneself, for what it truly is.

For some of us, the future appears to be an infinite field of potentiality. Since it has not happened yet, there is no telling what it might look like, meaning that there are any number of things we can do to bring a certain set of circumstances into being. From this perspective, it is a reflection of our total freedom or at least our perception of it.

Where this crosses over with aliens and UFOs is in what the alien makes us think of. We can not only see the Other and so get a better sense of *how* it is we see this Other, but we can also see what it looks like when a species gets such a firm grasp on its technology that the galaxy becomes its playground. Once we think of this, we ask the all-important question: How does the alien do this?

Perhaps it does this with an FTL (faster than light) drive. Or perhaps it has a device that can fold space-time, shortening the distance between points. It would need to eat along the way, so how does it store its food? Is there some manner of food preparation we have not developed yet that would allow it to stay preserved over long periods?

You see where this is going. True or not, the alien makes us think about what we might become, which sets us to work on figuring out how to become that thing. Science fiction has often imagined us as a space-faring species, along with many other alien races. This sounds like a good idea. The next step is figuring out how to make it practical.

But then there is the other transcendental move our minds make when thinking about alien life. Not just in terms of what future humanity might look like but also in how we might look to others. More to the point, where we are situated in the great cosmic narrative.

The most famous reflection on this theme is, of course, Carl Sagan's "Pale Blue Dot." The background of that writing is that the Voyager 1 space probe had traveled a distance of four billion miles from its home planet, Earth. Sagan, a popularizer of science (almost like a Neil Degrasse Tyson of his day), suggested that NASA turn Voyager's camera around to take a picture of Earth from that distance.

The result was one of the more dramatic and humbling pictures ever taken. In it, Earth is so small that it appears as nothing more than a pale blue dot—almost, it seems, too small to see.

But, as Sagan pointed out, despite being so tiny, that pale blue dot is our home (Sagan, 1997). It is where the history of our people occurred, everything from the rise of Julius Caesar to the life and work of Isaac Newton to Shakespeare, and everything that has ever happened within and throughout every culture that has ever walked on Earth.

Consider then that this picture is of Earth from four billion miles away. How big is the observable universe, exactly? Well, some estimates say that it is about 5.467×10^23 miles in diameter—about 93 billion lightyears (NASA, 2014.). From most points in the universe, the Earth would be so far away as to be invisible to the naked eye.

When we imagine life that can traverse the galaxy, we are imagining life from worlds so far away that we cannot see their host planet. We have to imagine for an instant just how big the universe is and just how small a human being is within it. As we do, the size and scope of reality becomes not just unfathomable but crushingly so.

Whether this is understood in positive or negative terms is, perhaps, dependent upon the individual. On the positive side, we can say that this is humbling—that it puts our needs and desires into perspective and reminds us of just how many more things there are in the universe than us and what afflicts us. What use is it to worry about a personal slight or a lost opportunity when there is so much more to the world than just this? Why focus inward and see ourselves as the center of things when it is so obvious that we are not?

On the other hand, perhaps the scale of things is a source of terror. For Lovecraft, it was. When he looked out at the stars, he saw not only that he was insignificant—he saw that what was out there did not care about him. The universe was not alive with possibility but utterly dead and horrifying. That he represented the world through forces of cosmic indifference, alien and beyond comprehension, shows just what thinking of the universe did to him.

Do we see the same thing? Do we see a material world in which life is a tale told by an idiot, full of sound and fury, signifying nothing?

This is not the place to settle this argument. Instead, we should only say that whether we feel exaltation or dread at the scope of the universe, contemplating other worlds and the life that lives on them brings the vastness of the cosmos into focus and reminds us of what we really are.

Returning to our earlier point: Not only does it do that, but it reminds us of *what we might be.*

Chapter 17:

The Future of Unidentified—New Frontiers in Extraterrestrial Research

Technology is advancing in ways we could not have imagined, even just a few years ago. Part of this is because of private companies, part of it because of public ventures like the military. But whatever the cause, there is no doubt that in the very near future, things will look substantially different from how they look now.

Already we have seen incredible advances not just in medicine, but in communications, video technology, batteries, and a whole host of other things. In many ways, life is becoming indistinguishable from the science fiction we spoke about in the last chapter.

All of this has implications for the search for extraterrestrial life.

What will happen when we become a multiplanet species? What about when we can augment our bodies to withstand the G-force from a ship traveling three-quarters of the speed of light? When we can live hundreds of years, thus, making the distance between solar systems that much smaller?

What about our ability to research our home world? If there are things visiting us from other planets, and we can detect signatures that may have been previously invisible to us, where will they hide?

This may sound fanciful. But research in the areas of human augmentation, brain-computer interfaces, and space travel have all indicated that in the not-so-distant future, we may find that distance no longer becomes an obstacle—and that whatever is out, *whoever* is out there, will no longer be relegated to the deepest parts of our imaginations.

Traversing The Cosmos

There was a time, especially in the '60s after the first moon landing, when it seemed obvious that NASA would lead the way toward us becoming a multiplanet species. Rocket technology had gotten to the point where we could put men on the moon and then bring them back unscathed. Since that was over such a short period of time, it was clear to anyone and everyone that this would only continue unabated until we were as scattered throughout the galaxy as in Asimov's *Foundation*.

It has been a long time since the last moon landing. NASA's manned space program entered a decades-long period of neglect (Kaku, 2018), during which time public support for space travel fell.

But in recent years, that began to change. In 2015, NASA announced that it had begun plans to send humans to Mars. They also put together a number of other goals for themselves, including returning to the moon.

NASA, in other words, was back—and was getting serious, once again, about the prospect of colonizing other worlds.

How this happened was due to a variety of factors. One that cannot go unmentioned is the influence Hollywood and television have on the public's perception of the endeavor. But in addition to this, private companies like SpaceX and Blue Origin have given rise to the idea that it was time to bring back sending people out into the stars.

SpaceX in particular, led by Elon Musk, has set its sights on going to Mars, with Musk saying that he wants to colonize the planet in his lifetime. Meanwhile, Bezos' Blue Origin is slightly less ambitious in its goals of going back to the moon—although this too is a welcome development.

Because these companies, each of them led by multi-billionaires, have enough money in them to encourage innovation and development, in addition to the company mandate to begin the colonization of other worlds, the rest of the space industry has had the opportunity to piggyback off their developments and kickstart their own missions into space. For example, because of developments in rocket technology, the rockets themselves have gotten cheaper. Because of this, NASA's excursions into the cosmos will no longer come with as hefty a price tag as they once did, making it less likely that they incur the wrath of penny-pinching taxpayers.

In other words, this sudden influx of private development has perhaps kickstarted a new era of spacefaring, bringing us one step closer to meeting other species on other worlds.

But before we do that, there is one question we should be asking:

Do we want to?

What Kind Of Life?

In the classic film *Alien*, a group of blue-collar workers on a huge shipping vessel in outer space come across a signal from another planet.

Is it an SOS? A warning? It does not really matter—they have been given a directive to investigate all possibilities of alien life on their journey lest they forfeit their shares in the company, meaning they do not get paid.

They have no choice—they have to land and see where the signal is coming from.

What they find down there is the stuff of cinematic legend. A long-dead race of aliens with technology that seems to have come from a demented imagination. Strange pods all along the ground. Of course, the thing that incubates in those pods: The most terrifying creature man has ever known.

Alien brings together a number of different, very primal fears into one setting. The titular alien begins its life as a "face-hugger" that impregnates people forcefully through the mouth; it changes quickly and unpredictably; and it *hunts* the people of the ship, who are trapped aboard in the middle of space, with no one nearby who can help them.

In a way, this is not so fantastical a situation. We do not know the nature of life out there on other worlds. Even if we were to encounter dozens of peaceful ones, that does not mean there is nothing out there that far exceeds our wildest nightmares. In fact, it is almost certain that something out there does match that description.

How sure are we that we want to risk running into something like that? Should we really publicize the fact that we are here, on this planet? What if *something* out there notices us that we would rather have just passed us by?

It would be like one of those scenes from slasher movies: Someone hidden in a cupboard, trying not to make a sound, while outside, and just barely visible, the hulking monstrosity looks around for them, knife in hand, ready to kill.

Yet, would it not be possible that some of these species are peaceful? Perhaps they had doggedly pursued knowledge in order to bring peace and security to their species instead of as a method to kill and exploit one another. Perhaps they see themselves in a fashion that we cannot comprehend, with motives that are difficult to translate. Perhaps they do not have an interest in spacefaring at all but prefer to stay on their homeworld and, it seems, entertain guests.

Since we do not know of any alien species in existence, we can only speculate as to the kinds of things that might be out there. But considering the likelihood that at least one of them is a creature drawn from the deepest wells of horror, it seems that we should try and be prepared, at the very least.

Yet, this is precisely where we encounter a significant problem. An alien creature that is primitive and hostile might be easy to defend against, given that, if nothing else, humans are exceptionally good at building weapons. But what if the species is more advanced than we are?

It would be delusional to think that we can be plucky and resourceful enough to beat something that is smarter and more violent than we are. This would be tantamount to asserting that we can beat a gorilla at arm-wrestling.

So how do we prepare for the possibility of meeting a hostile alien force? And what are its implications for space travel?

Singularity

Technology is not only being developed more quickly than at previous times, but the speed at which it is being developed is itself increasing. This means that we are making more new things in shorter periods of time, which means too that it is difficult, if not impossible, to imagine what the future might look like.

This is roughly the idea of a hypothetical moment called the "Singularity." In effect, it is like the singularity of a black hole, which is a point of no return, after which you sink into the black hole, into the ultimate unknown. The singularity here means that technology would be so advanced on the other side of this moment, that the future is like that black hole: A total unknown, impossible to predict.

The most famous proponent of the singularity is a man named Ray Kurzweil. In his mammoth book *The Singularity Is Near: When Humans Transcend Biology*, he states that one of the key moments—perhaps *the* key moment—in the move toward singularity is when we build an AI that has greater-than-human intelligence (Kurzweil, 2005). When this happens, the rate of technological change will become much more rapid, as this AI will be responsible for creating our new technologies. This would perhaps lead to the creation, by the AI, of even *more* advanced intelligence, thus speeding up the process to an unimaginable degree.

One other of these future developments, as Kurzweil sees it, will be the integration of man with machine. Biology is, of course, severely limited. We are liable to pain and injury; we need to eat, we need to sleep, and, all things considered, we do not live for an exceptionally long time.

This can all be changed by virtue of becoming post-human—meaning, that we become so integrated with machine technology that we become *something else.*

In particular, we can increase our intelligence by allowing for what are called BCIs (brain-computer interfaces), but specifically by creating BCIs that are designed to increase our general intelligence. Already, we use them for all manner of things, including sending commands to robots (Kurzweil, 2005). In fact, since *The Singularity Is Near* was published, incredible advances have been made with BCIs that could, if they continue on this trajectory, make physical disability a thing of the past.

However, in the event that we do use them to become more intelligent, this has several implications. First, we will not be so reliant on the superintelligent AI to do all of our thinking for us (although it will probably still do most of it). so we will become better at developing technologies that allow us to solve the problem of, say, building a ship that can go from Earth to the furthest reaches of space.

For our purposes, however, it can also help us plan against an attack by a technologically advanced alien race.

This particular angle is not something Kurzweil concerns himself with. But the idea of taking our own advancement into our own hands, and developing technologies that allow us to transcend our limitations does lend itself as a possible solution to many of these problems—even as it suggests other, greater problems that may be waiting for us.

To begin with, by making ourselves more advanced and not relying on the slow pace of evolution to do this for us, we increase the odds that *we* are the most advanced species in the galaxy. Meaning that if and when we do find something out there that is hostile and possesses weapons we cannot imagine *now* if we are the kind of animal that *can* create advanced defense systems *at this moment*, then we are in a good position to defend ourselves if and when we have to.

This might sound like something out of a bad military sci-fi novel, but there is truth to the idea that singularity may have some utility here. If we keep putting out signals that we are here, in this corner of the Milky Way, and of a certain level of advancement, the last thing we would want is to laugh at the idea that we become attacked by bug creatures from *Starship Troopers*, only to find out that this is precisely what was coming for us all along.

But then there is a further question about alien life that is suggested by this topic. It is an obvious one, although perhaps more horrifying than we might be comfortable admitting at first.

And that is: *What if the aliens out there have already reached singularity themselves?*

Machine Creatures From Mars

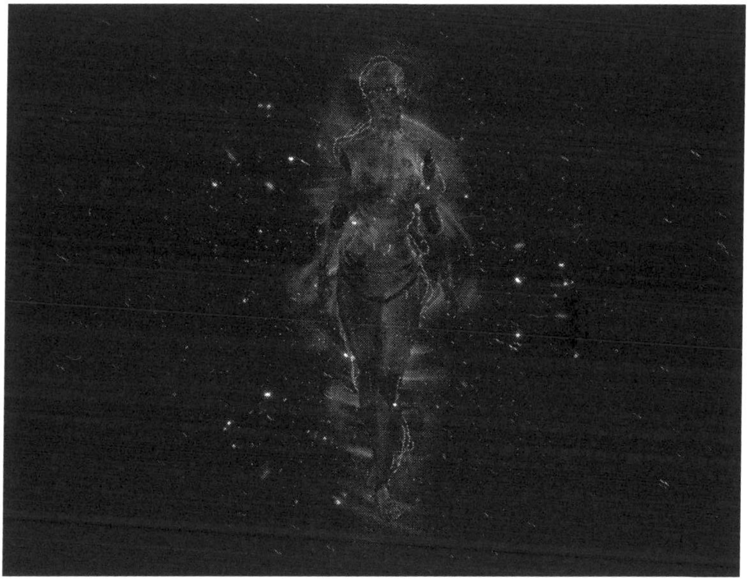

In the chapter on Roswell, we went over a claim that scientists had the body of an extraterrestrial from the crash and that they had performed an autopsy on it. One of the discovers allegedly made by one of the doctors was that the alien's body seemed well-suited for space travel—meaning that it appeared to have a system that allowed it to live for long periods of time, perhaps withstand the stress of space travel, and even use its psychic abilities to pilot the ship.

Whether or not this is true, the point to take away from it is that not all bodies are able to survive the kinds of travel we are thinking about here. Furthermore, some of the maneuvers we have said UFOs allegedly make—like the sharp, 90-degree turns—would probably turn most life forms into a grotesque pile of, frankly, guts.

Since many of these problems are baked into the laws of physics, they are not themselves solvable. There really is only so much stress a body can be put under before it sustains lethal amounts of damage, for example. So, too, is it that people need a certain amount of food, which requires space. So when you are designing a ship for that type of travel, you need to be mindful of the fact that it should be made in such a way that it kills all the passengers and also that it has enough space for food and water, in addition to the other amenities we require.

The solution in some ways seems obvious: You cannot change the laws of nature, so why not change the human being? If we can be augmented to withstand the pressure of increased G-force, then why not? If we can use nanotechnology to keep our bodies intact while reducing our need for food—why not?

If we find ourselves visited by a species from across the galaxy, it is more than likely that they will have enhanced themselves in this and similar ways. There is little chance that they have the kind of biology that allows for long space travel since nothing could have possibly evolved to do so—unless it was made in a lab, which, ultimately, is maybe not impossible.

The question then is: How do we prepare for such a species if they find us first? What can we do about singularized aliens with minds that surpass our smartest people by several orders of magnitude?

The answer, of course, is that we have no idea. In order to answer that question, we would need something to experiment on—we would need, in other words, an alien life form that has passed through the singularity. Since we do not even know if that exists, all we can do for now is speculate.

Furthermore, there is very little chance any of us could convince private donors, let alone our governments, to direct funding toward something so theoretical. With no information at our disposal, any scenario we conjure up with regard to a hostile first contact will be so speculative that it might as well be considered a dream.

That said, we should not allow ourselves to be deluded by some of the solutions to alien invasions proposed by Hollywood or even some of our literary works on the subject. We cannot, for example, upload a computer virus into their mothership since a computer virus is designed to affect a specific operating system, which the aliens would clearly not possess. We cannot wait for them to become sick with one of our pathogens either since, like the computer virus, our pathogens have emerged through a symbiotic relationship with life on Earth—in other words, there is no chance that alien biology could become sick with our common cold.

It is likely true that the best we can do is to allow technology to merge with us so that we become enhanced enough to have some level of a chance against a hostile force. Again, this is as theoretical a discussion as one can imagine, since we do not even know if alien life exists. But in the event that we do find one that is intent on resorting to violence, the hope would be, despite their ability to travel between stars, that we are somehow more advanced than them.

The Cold War

Then, there is the issue of international cooperation.

Many countries now have a space program. It is no longer the sole domain of the United States and the Soviet Union but includes Europe and China, among others. Theoretically, this would mean that more minds are contributing to innovation, sharing their findings, and helping each other better prepare for the possibility of first contact.

The issue, however, is that a Second Cold War has broken out. The "teams" are largely the same as they were last time, with the United States, Europe, Canada, and Australia on one side and on the other, a new Eastern axis led by China, along with Russia and Iran.

On the one hand, this scenario may provide a framework in which each "side" competes with the other, leading to a version of the space race with more advanced technology. Such were the conditions that led to our first excursions beyond the atmosphere—perhaps they are repeatable.

But the level of secrecy and paranoia that goes on during a Cold War might mean that some of our technologies get redirected toward more warlike ends.

For example, advanced AI could be used to come up with a novel method for detecting alien communications in the event that they do not use radio. This could allow us to pinpoint approximately where they are in space and perhaps even come up with a plan for how to address their existence.

But if the pressure being put on us is to create AI systems that develop offensive and/or defensive initiatives—say, to help combat a Chinese takeover of Taiwan or Japan—then those resources are tied up. In other words, an invention that could be used for knowledge gathering and exploration finds itself turned into a weapon of war, thus making it less likely that we find our alien neighbors at all.

The best we can hope for is clearly an end to the Second Cold War and a new era of cooperation. If that is too pie-in-the-sky, then maybe the best thing that can happen is we push each other through the sheer drive to win, such that someone, somewhere, comes up with the device that shows us, finally, that we are not alone.

Re: Evaluate

What will happen to us when we *do* finally meet our galactic neighbors?

What will that do to our sense of ourselves and our place in the universe? Will we find ourselves knocked off our pedestals, rooting around aimlessly like lost souls in a Beckett play? Will we find ourselves energized by possibilities, looking toward our future with the first optimistic eye in a long, long time?

Will a hostile alien force make us rethink whether the Enlightenment was a project toward peacefulness and reason? Or will it make us rethink the nature of rationality itself—perhaps that it is not a means for understanding the world but a means for violently extracting resources or experiencing the thrill of combat?

So much of our sense of self comes from being at the top of the pile. There are animals who can best us in physical combat, but none can out-think us. We have devised tools to help us compete with the other animals and preserve our own lives when all we have, really, are frail bodies, without much muscle, and a skin that is as soft and penetrable as butter.

This has given us an image of ourselves as the masters of this planet. We have often written about human beings as the animals through which history happens, as the things that are destined to become like gods, and make the world in its image. This may or may not be true, but that is beside the point. The point is rather that maybe we see ourselves in this way because of our uncontestedness.

In *The Dark Knight Rises*, Batman encounters the villain Bane for the first time in what appears to be a sewer. Batman pulls everything out of his bag of tricks to best the terrorist fanatic, but Bane is unperturbed.

The scene ends with Bane lifting Batman into the air and bringing him down on his knee. Batman's back becomes dislocated, effectively making him useless.

But before Bane performs this act on Batman, he says something quite profound. He says, "Victory has defeated you."

Batman is vulnerable because he lacks the animal instinct to survive. He has bested everyone that has come his way, and it has made him lose what is most primal in him. Because of this, Bane is able to get the upper hand, and nearly kills him as a result.

A similar scenario could play out in the event that we encounter an alien species. If the aliens are hostile, it could be that we will be unready for whatever they throw at us. But even if they are friendly, a similar level of shakiness could result from that encounter.

How will we react to that sense of being shaken? Will it cause us to slink off into the darkness, reevaluate our place in the universe, develop new systems of thought to cope with this information, and then emerge from the shadows, reinvigorated, ready to deal with the new paradigm?

Or will we take their level of advancement as a challenge—and see which one of us is left standing?

***

Human-machine integration, first contact with advanced lifeforms and interplanetary warfare are, in some ways, the final moments of our history, the culmination of everything we have prepared for.

These are the moments when science fiction becomes life. We see this around us all the time, from when we use AI for research to when a voice in our car tells us to make a turn to when we hear that a billionaire plans to colonize Mars, and soon.

Since our earliest stories we have wondered about what it would be like to encounter beings from elsewhere. Now that doing so is no longer unthinkable, and we find ourselves asking not *if* we can reach other planets, but *how*—then, at that point, we are bring myths to life.

But whatever the dangers, whatever the obstacles, it increasingly seems as though technology and mutual, international cooperation are the keys to bringing ourselves out into the stars.

If only because, more likely than not, it is what allowed them to come to us.

Conclusion

As we stand on the brink of interstellar exploration, the historical chronicles of UFO encounters remind us that the unknown may not be as distant as we think. But what lessons can we carry into the future?

Will we, like our ancient ancestors, worship the beings we find as gods? Will we treat them as enemies or as objects of scientific inquiry? Will we see them as angels, possessing the keys to our return to Eden?

Will we learn from them? Compete with them?

How much will knowing they are out there change things down here?

During every epoch of human history, the strange and unexplained things in the sky have always *meant* something to us. During our earliest days, a light so bright it appeared as if another moon was seen as a sign that the gods had made themselves known through the fabric of reality. For us now, the lights are signs that maybe our wildest speculations about the future really could come true.

Is this what we should take with us as we venture to explore space—that the unknown and the mysterious are always signs of possibility? That they are a receptacle of our dreams and fantasies?

Is the UFO always a sign that we should look inward?

What does it mean, after all, that through these stories—of UFO encounters and meetings with creatures from other planets—we see ourselves not just as observers of the universe, but as something that is observed? Perhaps this is connected to some of our religious intuitions, of experiencing the ever-watchful eye of God, only now updated for the science fictional century, and *centuries* ahead.

Are we finally seeing ourselves in proportion to the world around us? Are we getting a sense of ourselves not as the apex predator but as a bit player in an enormous cosmic drama?

Going out into the universe is not going to make these thoughts go away. Sure, by then, we will have conquered distance as an obstacle as we become able to shoot between stars at awe-inspiring speeds. But as the universe becomes more accessible to us, we will not have to merely imagine its size but experience it first-hand. This is because learning is a realization of the extent of your ignorance. Study is a means not of gaining knowledge but humility.

Our relationship with UFOs, then, is a millennia-long exercise in humility. It is a means for coming to terms with our smallness, the sheer number of possibilities in the universe, and the realization of how far we have yet to go if we want to be masters of our own destinies.

Maybe this is the lesson we carry into the future: No matter how far we have come, there is always further to go.

And further. And further still.

***

But are they really out there?

On the one hand, we cannot delude ourselves with wishful thinking. There is nothing in the way of concrete evidence to suggest that alien spacecraft are shooting through our skies.

The suggestion has been brought up plenty of times, and plenty of investigations have gone deep to get answers.

Every single time, however, the answer is the same: People mistake terrestrial for extraterrestrial phenomena, and interpret it according to our cultural anxieties, but there really is nothing out there. Nothing has visited us from other planets, no aircraft is making impossible maneuvers—nothing.

So what do we do with all those testimonies, then? What about the man who says he spoke to people who saw an alien get shot and killed at Roswell? What about the abductions, the independent eyewitnesses in Belgium, the whole cities of Phoenix and Tehran seeing something that hovered over their homes that appeared on radar?

Not only those but there is the way the entire history of humanity seems to have run into these objects. Medieval soldiers who saw "shields" floating in the sky, the possibility that the Bible contains UFOs—have we not just looked over an entire history of our people bumping into flying vehicles?

The only response is: *Have we?*

At every turn, we have encountered strange things in the sky. We have read stories told by people to other people, who finally told someone who wrote it down. Still, some of the stories we read are staggeringly old, meaning the number of telephone game stations leading up to now might as well be a billion.

These are merely hints and whispers. Some of these whispers appear in forms much like urban legends, others like myths, or prophecies. Always, we look to them for evidence that we, right now, are correct, and that the signs have been right there in front of us all along.

In the Bible, Ezekiel encounters vehicles that are like wheels within wheels, as well as creatures with multiple heads who come down from the sky. Are these aliens? We might interpret them as such, given our cultural expectations. Still others might say that Ezekiel was schizophrenic, or had ingested ergot fungus and hallucinated.

But then, maybe Ezekiel is describing the sheer alienness of the world beyond. Maybe he decided to use poetic language to show that the world was not a human one, but something utterly alien—not in a science fictional sense, but in the sense that it is foreign and strange. If that is the case, then reading aliens into the text is a far too literal reading of a blatantly metaphorical story—and, therefore, misses the point of the text completely.

In other words, reinterpreting our religions in such a way as to prove they are about aliens is nothing more than a reductionist method that flattens out the complexity of ancient myths. Maybe what we should do instead, is to allow for the enormous complexities, the ambiguities and the unknowns, to manifest themselves as they are: an enormous field of possibility.

***

But we should not let this stop us.

Curiosity is not a destination. It is both a question and an answer. It is self-justified. The object is not to arrive at the truth but to propel oneself forward in a quixotic pursuit for it.

That we still want to find life on other worlds or other beings that exist alongside us; that we still wonder aloud if there are other dimensions, psychic powers, and technology that borders on magic; and that we recognize, albeit implicitly, that there are always forces greater than us—these are the signs of a species that has not yet given up. It is a sign of a working imagination, of a willingness to think outside the box, no matter how crazy.

If the UFO phenomenon really is nothing more than a present-day mythology, then it takes place among the grand mythologies of history, as a source of wonder, and as a message from our unconscious to our conscious brains, that there we have not exhausted our possibilities. There is always something greater, and greater, and greater still.

In the pursuit of understanding UFOs, we uncover not just unexplained phenomena but the reflection of humanity's enduring quest for knowledge, connection, and our place within the cosmic tapestry.

Perhaps, then, it is the perfect myth for our time.

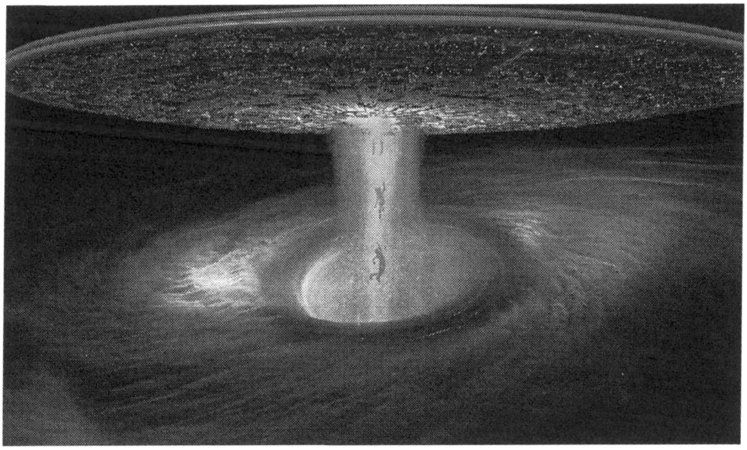

If you enjoyed the read, it would be great if you could leave a review, links are over the page. Thanks so much, I appreciate your feedback and support.

US Review Link

UK Review Link

Canada Review Link

References

ABC News. (2010, July 14). *UFO in China's skies prompts investigation.* ABC News. https://abcnews.go.com/International/ufo-china-closes-airport-prompts-investigation/story?id=11159531

Amond, A., De Brouwer, W., Ferryn, P., & Meessen, A. (n.d.). *ERNAGE 1989: The facts and their analysis.* http://www.cobeps.org/pdf/ernage_rapport_old.pdf

Anton, A., & Vugrin, F. (2022). "UFOs exist and everyone needs to adjust to that fact." (Dis)information campaigns on the UFO phenomenon. *Journal of Anomalistics*, *22*, 18–35.

Artnet News. (October 14, 2023). *Is there a UFO in that Renaissance painting? See 7 historical artworks that (possibly) depict close encounters with the third kind.* artnet. https://news.artnet.com/art-world-archives/aliens-ufos-in-art-historical-paintings-2350998

Aquinas, T. (2020). *Summa theoligicae in Delphi collected works of Thomas Aquinas.* Delphi Classics.

Bauer, C. (2016). *Tunguska.* Createspace Independent Publishing Platform.

Beasley, W. H., & Tinsley, B. A. (1974). Tungus event was not caused by a black hole. *Nature*, *250*(5467), 555–556. https://doi.org/10.1038/250555a0

KCAL News. (2020, April 28). *Pentagon declassifies 3 UFO videos after Blink 182's Tom DeLonge leaked them*. CBSnews. https://www.cbsnews.com/losangeles/news/pentagon-declassifies-3-ufo-videos-after-blink-182s-tom-delonge-leaked-them/

Chester, K. (2007). *Strange company: Military encounters with ufos in world war II*. Anomalist Books.

Colavito, J. (2012, December 12). *The UFO battle over nuremburg*. JASON COLAVITO. https://www.jasoncolavito.com/blog/the-ufo-battle-over-nuremburg

Corso, P., & Birnes, W. J. (1998). *The day after Roswell*. Simon and Schuster.

De Brouwer, W. (2010). *UFOs: Generals, pilots, and government officials go on the record* (p. Chapter 2). Random House Inc.

Downing, B. (1973). *The Bible and flying saucers*. Da Capo Press.

Drolia, R. (2014, July 15). *10,000-year-old rock paintings depicting aliens and ufos found in chhattisgarh*. The Times of India. https://timesofindia.indiatimes.com/india/10000-year-old-rock-paintings-depicting-aliens-and-UFOs-found-in-Chhattisgarh/articleshow/38435091.cms

Duda, J. (2024, March 13). *Phoenix Lights became Arizona UFO legend in 1997*. Axios Pheonix. https://www.axios.com/local/phoenix/2024/03/13/lights-arizona-ufo-legend-1997

Grusch, D. (n.d.). *Opening statement*. https://oversight.house.gov/wp-content/uploads/2023/07/Dave_G_HOC_Speech_FINAL_For_Trans.pdf

Gupta, M. (2021, November 15). *What is a camera now?* College of Letters and Science. https://ls.wisc.edu/news/what-is-a-camera-now

Harvey, A. (2024, May 11). *Aliens, strange aircrafts, and mysterious infections: Inside the varginha UFO incident of 1996.* All That's Interesting. https://allthatsinteresting.com/varginha-ufo-incident

Hastings, R. (2006). *UFO sightings at ICBM sites and nuclear weapons storage areas.* nicap. http://www.nicap.org/babylon/missile_incidents.htm

Hirshberg, P. (n.d.). *First the media, then us: How the internet changed the fundamental nature of the communication and its relationship with the audience.* BBVA Open Mind. https://www.bbvaopenmind.com/wp-content/uploads/2014/04/BBVA-OpenMind-First-the-Media-Then-Us-How-Internet-Changed-Fundamental-Nature-of-Communication-and-its-relationship-whit-audience-Peter-Hirsberg.pdf.pdf

History.com Editors. (2017, December 4). *Nazca lines.* HISTORY; A&E Television Networks. https://www.history.com/topics/south-america/nazca-lines

Huneeus, A. (2010, May 16). *Ancient Chinese UFO records.* Open Minds: Credible UFO News and Information. https://openminds.tv/chinese-ufo-records/

Icke, D. (2000). *The biggest secret.* Bridge Of Love.

Danelek, J. A . (2010). *The great airship of 1897.* SCB Distributors.

Javier, F., & Natera, M. (2012). *Coyame: A history of the American settler.* Xlibris Corporation.

Kaku, M. (2018). *The future of humanity: Terraforming Mars, interstellar travel, immortality, and our destiny beyond Earth.* Doubleday, A Division Of Penguin Random House Llc.

Kean, L. (2010). UFOs : generals, pilots, and government officials go on the record. Harmony Books.

Klein, C. (2016, January 9). *America's First UFO Sighting.* HISTORY. https://www.history.com/news/americas-first-ufo-sighting

KTAR.com. (2017, June 14). *Was actor Kurt Russell the pilot who reported the Phoenix Lights?* KTAR.com. https://ktar.com/story/1619900/actor-kurt-russell-claims-pilot-report-phoenix-lights/

KTAR.com. (2019, March 13). *More than 20 years later, mystery of Phoenix Lights still fascinates people.* KTAR.com. https://ktar.com/story/1490163/more-than-20-years-later-mystery-of-phoenix-lights-still-fascinates-people/

Kurczy, S. (2010, July 16). *China UFO spotted again. Why skepticism is warranted.* Christian Science Monitor. https://www.csmonitor.com/World/Global-News/2010/0716/China-UFO-spotted-again.-Why-skepticism-is-warranted

Kurzweil, R. (2005). *The singularity is near: When humans transcend biology.* Duckworth.

Liu, J. (2013, February 13). *The global Catholic population.* Pew Research Center's Religion & Public Life Project. https://www.pewresearch.org/religion/2013/02/13/the-global-catholic-population/

Lomas, T. (2024). A history of scientific approaches to unidentified anomalous phenomena: Time to rethink their relegation to the paranormal and engage seriously? Journal of Scientific Exploration, 38(1), 91–109. https://doi.org/10.31275/20243163

Mack, J. E. (1999). *Passport to the cosmos.* Three Rivers Press (CA).

Magee, J. M. (2020, February 4). *Angels.* Thomistic Philosophy Page. https://aquinasonline.com/angels/#:~:text=For

NASA. (2014, January 24). *WMAP- Shape of the universe.* National Aeronautics and Space Administration. https://map.gsfc.nasa.gov/universe/uni_shape.html

Oberg, J. (1978). *Tunguska echoes.* The Skeptical Inquirer. https://cdn.centerforinquiry.org/wp-content/uploads/sites/29/1979/01/22165456/p51.pdf

Pasulka, D. W. (2023). *Living folk religions.* Taylor & Francis.

Picknett, L., & Prince, C. (1999). *Stargate conspiracy.* Hachette UK.

Platov, Yu. V., & Sokolov, B. A. (2000). The study of unidentified flying objects in the soviet union. *Herald of the Russian Academy of Sciences*, *70*(3), 244–251.

Rahman, K. R. (2023, February 12). *Now China says it has spotted a UFO.* Newsweek. https://www.newsweek.com/china-says-spotted-unidentified-flying-object-ufo-1780648

Readman, K. (2024, January 22). *Project Blue Book: What did the US conclude about UFOs?* Historic Mysteries. https://www.historicmysteries.com/history/project-blue-book/38902/

Robinson, W. G. (1997). Heaven's Gate: The end. *Journal of Computer-Mediated Communication, 3*(3). https://doi.org/10.1111/j.1083-6101.1997.tb00077.x

Romo, V., & Chappell, B. (2023, July 27). *U.S. recovered non-human "biologics" from UFO crash sites, former intel official says.* NPR; NPR. https://www.npr.org/2023/07/27/1190390376/ufo-hearing-non-human-biologics-uaps

Ruppelt, E. J. (2023). *The report on unidentified flying objects.* Double 9 Books.

Sagan, C. (1997). *Pale blue dot: A vision of the human future in space.* Ballantine Books. (Original work published 1994)

Salla, M. (2005). *A report on the motivations and activities of extraterrestrial races - A typology of the most significant extraterrestrial races interacting with humanity.* http://www.vielewelten.at/pdf_en/report%20on%20the%20motivations.pdf

Saywitz, K. J. (1988). The credibility of child witnesses. *Family Advocate, 10*(3), 38–41. https://www.jstor.org/stable/25804590?read-now=1&seq=3#page_scan_tab_contents

Schiele, A. (2020). Pseudoscience as media effect. *Journal of Science Communication, 19*(02). https://doi.org/10.22323/2.19020101

Shermer, M. (2021). Unidentified: Are UFOs and UAPs ordinary, extraordinary terrestrial, or extraordinary extraterrestrial phenomena? *Skeptic Magazine, 26*(3), 16–24.

Smith, J. C. (2004, July 24). *The Mexican Air Force UFO affair: Aliens, ball lightning, or flares?* Skeptic.

https://www.skeptic.com/eskeptic/04-07-24/#mexiUFO

Specktor, B. (2022, July 22). *The Pentagon is officially opening a UFO investigation office.* Livescience. https://www.livescience.com/pentagon-ufo-sighting-office

Stables, D. (2021, August 23). *England's crop circle controversy.* BBC. https://www.bbc.com/travel/article/20210822-englands-crop-circle-controversy

Statistica. (2023). *Crimes in Mexico City by type 2022.* Statista. https://www.statista.com/statistics/1288398/crimes-mexico-city-by-type/#:~:text=The

Steiger, B. (2019). *Project blue book: The top secret UFO files that revealed a government cover-up.* Mufon.

Stise, R., Bingaman, J., Aysha Siddika, Dawson, W., Paintsil, A., & Brewer, P. R. (2023). Cultivating paranormal beliefs: how television viewing, social media use, and podcast listening predict belief in UFOs. *Atlantic Journal of Communication,* 1–14. https://doi.org/10.1080/15456870.2023.2187803

Tanaka, K. (2020, June 26). *"Utsurobune": A UFO legend from nineteenth-century Japan.* Nippon.com. https://www.nippon.com/en/japan-topics/g00879/

Tedesco, E. F. (2024, May 10). *Tunguska event: Summary, cause, & facts.* Britannica. https://www.britannica.com/event/Tunguska-event#ref182568

Theunredacted. (2016, March 10). *The Tunguska blast: Tesla's death ray.* Theunredacted.com.

https://theunredacted.com/the-tunguska-blast-teslas-death-ray/

TIME. (1973, October 8). *Science: A black hole in Siberia?* TIME. https://time.com/archive/6841844/science-a-black-hole-in-siberia/

Tingley, B. (2024, March 8). *Pentagon UFO office finds "no empirical evidence" for alien technology in new report.* Space.com. https://www.space.com/pentagon-ufo-office-aaro-historical-report-no-emprical-evidence-alien-technology

Unidentified Phenomena. (2023, February 14). *The Tehran UFO incident (1976).* Unidentified Phenomena. https://unidentifiedphenomena.com/incidents/the-tehran-ufo-incident-1976/

Vallee, J., & Aubeck, C. (2010). *Wonders in the sky.* Penguin.

Von Däniken, E. (1968). *Chariots of the gods: unsolved mysteries of the past.* Berkley.

Webster, D. (2017, July 5). *In 1947, A high-altitude balloon crash landed in Roswell. the aliens never left.* Smithsonian; Smithsonian.com. https://www.smithsonianmag.com/smithsonian-institution/in-1947-high-altitude-balloon-crash-landed-roswell-aliens-never-left-180963917/

Wendt, A., & Duvall, R. (2011). *UFOs: Generals, pilots, and government officials go on the record* (p. Chapter 11). Random House Inc.

Wilson, P. (2022, June 12). Crop circles were made by supernatural forces. Named Doug and Dave. *The New York Times.* https://www.nytimes.com/2022/06/12/style/crop-circles.html

Image References

Antony, A. (2021). *They knows* [Image]. Unsplash. https://unsplash.com/photos/green-and-black-trees-under-blue-sky-HWQXIYbs8PM

Atelier, K. K. (2023). *Graf zeppelin over Bergen* [Image]. Unsplash. https://unsplash.com/photos/a-black-and-white-photo-of-an-airplane-in-the-sky-IUO3_Cs22cc

Jensen, D. (2017). *Climbing up from ocean* [Image]. Unsplash. https://unsplash.com/photos/closeup-photo-of-persons-hand-NMk1Vggt2hg

Jiang, D. (2019). *experimental shoot w/ model (alice)* [Image]. Unsplash. https://unsplash.com/photos/woman-in-black-crew-neck-shirt-oeZrm_Ea8v4

Kellepics. (2017a). *Fantasy, spirit, nightmare* [Image]. Unsplash. https://pixabay.com/photos/fantasy-spirit-nightmare-dream-2847724/

Kellepics. (2017b). *Fantasy UFO city image* [Image]. Unsplash. https://pixabay.com/photos/fantasy-ufo-city-science-fiction-2861815/

Leo_Visions. (2020). *Yosemite (Alien face)* [Image]. Unsplash. https://unsplash.com/photos/gray-scale-photo-of-human-face-sMPRCsoUM4A

LunarSeaArt. (2017). *Demon* [Image]. Pixabay. https://pixabay.com/photos/devil-horns-demon-satan-black-2374369/

Meyers, D. (2019). *Nuclear plant panel* [Image]. Unsplash. https://unsplash.com/photos/gray-control-panel-cHR1Q2g1_F4

monikawl999. (2015). *Nazca lines* [Image]. Pixabay. https://pixabay.com/photos/nasca-peru-nasca-plateau-1089342/

Museums Victoria. (2019). *77 Squadron in the air* [Image]. Unsplash. https://unsplash.com/photos/three-monoplanes-squadron-in-world-war-2-oyGmigXV030

nutsch. (2019). *Tesla coil* [Image]. Pixabay. https://pixabay.com/photos/high-voltage-tesla-coil-electricity-4506065/

Pollio, S. (2017). *Hands, despair* [Image]. Unsplash. https://unsplash.com/photos/person-behind-fog-glass-ZC0EbdLC8G0

Studzinski, M. (2019). *Angel statue* [Image]. Unsplash. https://unsplash.com/photos/green-female-angel-statue-TEZLseYfyz0

TheDigitalArtist. (2018). *Android, science fiction* [Image]. Pixabay. https://pixabay.com/photos/android-science-fiction-cyborg-3080526/

Unrau, S. (2015). *Entering another dimension...* [Image]. Unsplash. https://unsplash.com/photos/trees-on-forest-with-sun-rays-sp-p7uuT0tw

Unsplash+. (2022). *Paint pouring, abstract* [Image]. Unsplash. https://unsplash.com/photos/a-computer-generated-image-of-an-abstract-design-3eCnjtgKwYw

Unsplash+. (2023). *UFO over city* [Image]. Unsplash. https://unsplash.com/photos/an-alien-flying-over-a-city-at-night-CadZjZPsDj0

Willgard. (2021). *Fantasy, spaceship* [Image]. Pixabay. https://pixabay.com/photos/fantasy-spaceship-science-fiction-6607469/

Zameshaev, D. (2022). *Helmet alien* [Image]. Unsplash. https://unsplash.com/photos/a-black-and-white-photo-of-a-man-in-the-dark-GsDm8AEVQ8k

Printed in Great Britain
by Amazon

484281ab-91c2-491e-9c90-49810a1c49e9R01